In the Shadow of Thunder

History of the City of Niagara Falls, New York

Mark Donnelly, PhD.

RPSS PUBLISHING
Buffalo, New York

Many thanks to the invaluable resources of the Niagara Falls Public Library, the Library of Congress, and the BN Arts & Culture photo archives, which provided much of the historical material used in this book. Numerous photographs and illustrations were digitally restored and enhanced to improve clarity and presentation.

RPSS Publishing, Buffalo New York

429 Englewood Avenue, Kenmore, NY 14223

rpsspublishing.com

drmaddog@hotmail.com.com

978-1-956688-71-9 Hardcover
In the Shadow of Thunder

Printed in the USA

RPSS PUBLISHING

This Book is Dedicated to:

The people who stayed.

The families who built lives in the shadow of turbines and smokestacks.

The mothers who knocked on doors when the ground would not stay silent.

The workers and neighbors who chose endurance over exit.

The Seneca Nation, whose presence here predates every survey line.

And to anyone who has ever stood at the railing,
felt the tremor beneath their feet,
and understood that living beside power
requires both humility and resolve.

The water keeps falling.

May we keep learning.

Table of Contents

A City in the Shadow of Thunder

Stand near the railing long enough and conversation becomes negotiation. The Falls do not quiet for you. They do not pause for emphasis. They speak in vapor and velocity.

Niagara Falls, New York has always lived with that sound.

Each year, millions arrive at this railing, lift their phones, and frame the cascade. Mist rises. Light refracts. Gravity performs on schedule. The image travels home with them, distilled into postcard certainty: Niagara Falls is a wonder.

It is.

But this book is not about the wonder alone.

It is about the rest of Niagara Falls.

Beyond the park boundary lies a city shaped not just by falling water, but by decisions made in its shadow. Streets laid out for factory workers. Brick corridors built for electrochemical ambition. Neighborhoods that absorbed both prosperity and pollution. Classrooms that opened even when headlines darkened. Border crossings that breathed with global politics. Sovereign land that never forgot its deeper history.

The roar has always been constant. The response has changed.

Niagara Falls, New York began as geology. Ice retreated. Rock yielded. Water found a ledge and kept finding it, inch by inch, century by century. Long before engineers diverted flow into turbines, the river was corridor and presence within the homelands of the Haudenosaunee Confederacy. Long before honeymooners arrived by rail, portage paths circled the cataract.

The Falls were never isolated. They were embedded in movement.

By the late nineteenth century, that movement turned electrical. Alternating current leapt from experiment to infrastructure. Hydropower translated thunder into wire. Factories rose along Buffalo Avenue. The skyline thickened with stacks and ambition. The city became a proving ground for modern industry.

Then came the Chemical Century.

Production intensified. Waste accumulated. Oversight lagged. Beneath backyards and schoolyards, buried decisions waited. When Love Canal surfaced into national consciousness, it did more than stain a neighborhood's name. It forced the country to reconsider what progress meant and who bore its cost.

Niagara Falls became cautionary tale without ceasing to be marvel.

Deindustrialization followed. Shift whistles quieted. Population declined. Downtown storefronts dimmed. Yet the turbines continued to spin at the Robert Moses Niagara Power Plant, operated by the New York Power Authority. The river never resigned.

Reinvention arrived in phases. Gaming under the banner of the Seneca Niagara Resort & Casino altered the skyline and economic

calculus. Renewable energy reframed hydropower from industrial backbone to climate asset. Cross-border life with Ontario evolved through policy shifts and shared illumination.

Through every cycle, one fact remained: the waterfall is not the whole story.

To write the history of Niagara Falls honestly is to write about leverage and liability, about spectacle and sewage, about turbines and treaties. It is to look past the mist and ask how a community lives beside immense force without being defined entirely by it.

The city has not always succeeded. It has not always been treated fairly by corporations or by broader economic currents. But it has persisted.

This book traces Niagara Falls in full: sacred corridor, frontier flashpoint, industrial crucible, environmental reckoning, border city, renewable engine. It seeks to restore proportion between postcard and pavement.

Niagara Falls, New York – from 1882 Map

ICE BUILT IT, WATER CLAIMED IT

Because the rest of Niagara Falls is not background.

It is the story.

Before there was a railing to lean against. Before there was a park map or a parking lot, there was pressure.

Twenty thousand years ago, ice sat over this region in sheets thick enough to erase hills and silence rivers. The glacier did not hurry. It pressed. It scoured. It carried rock like freight. What is now Niagara Falls, New York lay beneath a frozen weight that flattened forests and rerouted ancient waterways.

When the climate shifted and the ice began to retreat, it did not leave gently. It left rearranged.

Meltwater surged through newly carved channels, searching for the lowest path between Lake Erie and Lake Ontario. It found a ledge of resistant Dolostone resting atop softer shale. The river rushed forward, reached the lip, and dropped.

The first version of Niagara Falls was not where it stands today. The waterfall began miles downstream, near what is now Lewiston. Since then, it has been migrating upstream, eroding the softer rock beneath the capstone, collapsing sections of cliff, and inching backward in a slow geological retreat. The gorge is not scenery. It is autobiography written in stone.

Stand at the edge and you are looking at movement frozen mid-sentence.

The Niagara Escarpment is the quiet architect here. Its hard upper layer holds for a time. The softer layers beneath surrender. Water seeps into fractures, widens them through freeze and thaw, and eventually the overhang gives way. Entire sections of the Falls have collapsed in single thunderous events, altering the shape of the brink overnight. The process continues, moderated in the modern era by engineering controls, but never fully stilled.

Niagara Falls is not permanent. It is persistent.

Long before the arrival of European explorers, the river was a corridor of life. The region formed part of the homeland of the Haudenosaunee Confederacy, whose nations understood the river as artery and presence. The water connected inland forests to distant shores. It carried canoes, trade goods, and stories. The Falls themselves were not obstacles so much as thresholds, places of power embedded in a living landscape.

The sound would have been the same then. The mist rising from the plunge basin would have caught the sun in the same refracted light. But there were no souvenir stands, no daredevil plans sketched on napkins, no survey stakes marking parcels for speculation.

Only water negotiating gravity.

The Niagara River drains four of the five Great Lakes. It is not a modest stream. Roughly 85 percent of the surface freshwater in North America moves through this system. By the time it reaches the brink, the river is compressed between Goat Island and the mainland, accelerating through rapids before committing to the drop. The descent is not merely scenic. It is hydraulic force expressed at scale.

Geology shaped destiny here long before industry recognized the opportunity.

The shape of the gorge determined settlement patterns. The navigable river above the Falls invited trade. The impassable drop required portage. Trails developed around the cataract,

From James Hall, 1843, The Geology of New York,

embedding the location into regional movement. When European powers arrived in the seventeenth century, they encountered not wilderness, but a landscape already known, used, and named.

The word "Niagara"- likely derives from Indigenous language, often translated as "thundering waters." It is less a description than a condition. The sound is constant. It folds into daily life. Residents learn to speak over it, to sleep through it, to measure storms against it.

In winter, the Falls transform. Ice forms along the edges, building temporary cathedrals of white. Mist crystallizes on branches and railings. The river below can jam with slabs of frozen current, creating what nineteenth-century observers called an "ice bridge." Even then, the water continues beneath, patient and insistent.

This landscape did not invite fragility. It demanded adaptation.

The soil deposited by retreating glaciers proved fertile. Forests returned. Wildlife flourished. Human settlement followed patterns shaped by water access and defensible high ground. Over centuries, the gorge became not just geological feature but strategic asset. Whoever controlled the river corridor controlled movement between interior and coast.

But in the beginning, before forts and factories, there was simply the fact of the Falls.

They are young in geological terms. Twelve thousand years is a recent chapter in the planet's history. They are also dynamic. Without human intervention diverting portions of the flow for hydroelectric production, the rate of erosion would be faster. Engineering has slowed the retreat, stabilizing the brink. Even so, the underlying process continues. The gorge lengthens by increments measurable in inches over decades.

Niagara Falls is a reminder that landscapes are active.

To write the history of Niagara Falls, New York is to begin not with incorporation papers or industrial charters, but with ice. The city exists because a glacier retreated along a particular path. It exists because rock layers differ in hardness. It exists because gravity is patient.

Everything that follows, from tourism to turbines to environmental reckoning, is built atop that first arrangement of stone and current.

The Falls do not belong to the city. The city belongs to the Falls.

The Early Days of Niagara Falls

Long before Niagara Falls became a city, the thunder of water had already shaped the destiny of the land around it. The falls themselves were ancient, carved by glaciers thousands of years ago, but the human story along their banks unfolded gradually through exploration, trade, industry, and tourism.

Before European settlement, the Niagara region was home to the Neutral Nation, an Indigenous people who lived between the territories of the Iroquois and the Huron. The Neutral people used the Niagara River as part of a vital trade corridor linking the Great Lakes. The powerful rapids and the great waterfall forced travelers to carry their goods around the river's most dangerous sections along a portage trail. This path became one of the earliest transportation routes in the region.

When French explorers and missionaries arrived in the seventeenth century, they quickly recognized the strategic importance of the Niagara corridor. The Neutral Nation allowed the French and later the British to establish fortified outposts along the river. Among the most significant were Fort Niagara near the mouth of the river and Fort Schlosser near the upper portage above the falls. These forts protected trade routes and served as gateways between Lake Erie and Lake Ontario.

Even in these early years, the Niagara River was valued not only for transportation but also for its power. The French were the first Europeans to construct mills along the rapids, using the rushing water to grind grain and perform other mechanical work. The idea that Niagara's water could drive industry had taken root long before electricity transformed the landscape.

After the founding of the United States, land along the Niagara River became a valuable resource. Large portions of the riverbanks were auctioned off to private owners who envisioned factories and mills powered by the river's immense energy. One of the earliest promoters of this industrial potential was Augustus Porter, an entrepreneur and landowner who proposed constructing canals to divert water from the Niagara River to power mills and manufacturing.

Porter's ideas helped inspire later developments. By the mid-nineteenth century, engineers and investors were actively working to harness the river's power. In 1861, the Niagara Falls Hydraulic Power and Manufacturing Company completed the first canal designed specifically to feed water to industrial turbines. The canal marked the beginning of large-scale industrial development in the area.

Industry attracted workers, and workers attracted communities. Before the city of Niagara Falls officially existed, several small settlements developed near the river. Among them were the villages of Schlosser (also called Manchester), Niagara Falls, and Bellevue, later known as Suspension Bridge. These villages served the growing industries and the increasing number of visitors drawn by the spectacular waterfall.

Tourism was already becoming an important part of the local economy. Though travel in the early nineteenth century was difficult, improvements in transportation made Niagara Falls more accessible. Railroads reached the area by the mid-1800s, dramatically shortening travel times. A journey from New York City that once took weeks could now be completed in about 48 hours.

Village of Suspension Bridge

By 1850, roughly 80,000 tourists visited Niagara Falls each year, an astonishing number for the time. Visitors arrived to witness the natural wonder but often found themselves equally fascinated by the industrial activity along the river. The powerful tailraces of water discharged by mills and early power plants drew curious onlookers who marveled at the engineering that attempted to capture the falls' energy.

Hotels multiplied to accommodate the growing crowds. The American side of the falls quickly became the center of tourist activity, with dozens of hotels, shops, and attractions. Compared to the bustling streets and grand accommodations on the New York side, the Ontario shoreline remained relatively rural during these early years.

Transportation within the growing communities also improved. Beginning in 1882, streetcars connected neighborhoods, factories, and tourist attractions, eventually running as far as Buffalo. The electric rail system served both residents traveling to work and visitors moving between scenic viewpoints and hotels. Streetcars remained an essential part of city life until 1937.

By the time the City of Niagara Falls was officially incorporated in 1892, the region had already developed a strong identity shaped by both industry and tourism. The newly formed city combined the villages of Schlosser/Manchester, Niagara Falls, and Bellevue/Suspension Bridge into a single municipality with a population of just over 6,500 people.

The falls had already begun to transform the surrounding landscape. What had once been a wilderness portage trail used by Indigenous traders had become a place where factories, railroads, hotels, and neighborhoods grew beside one of the world's greatest natural wonders.

The city that emerged would spend the next century balancing two powerful forces: the beauty of the falls and the energy that flowed from them.

Where the Water Lives

The Ecology of Niagara Falls

Before it was industry, before it was honeymoon capital, Niagara was habitat.

The Niagara Falls ecosystem is not simply a waterfall. It is a massive, high-energy freshwater system powered by four Great Lakes. Water flows from Superior, Michigan, Huron, and Erie before plunging over the brink and continuing toward Lake Ontario. The Falls, the river, and the surrounding gorges form a living corridor–dynamic, biodiverse, and indispensable.

At its core is motion

The Niagara River, connecting Lake Erie to Lake Ontario, carries one of the largest flow rates of any river in North America relative to its length. That force shapes not only cliffs but communities of life. Fast currents oxygenate water, supporting diverse fish species. Deep pools and calmer stretches provide spawning and refuge zones. Among its most significant inhabitants is the endangered lake sturgeon, an ancient fish whose lineage predates the Falls themselves.

Niagara is a biodiversity hotspot. The region supports approximately 338 bird species, 35 mammals, 734 plant species, and numerous reptiles and amphibians. In winter, when much of the continent freezes, the open water below the Falls becomes sanctuary. The area is designated an Important Bird Area, hosting one of the most diverse concentrations of gulls in the world during the coldest months. Bald eagles perch along the gorge. Peregrine falcons nest on cliffs once carved by retreating glaciers.

On Goat Island alone, more than 600 species of flora thrive. The Niagara Gorge shelters rare plants that survive in microclimates created by mist, shade, and escarpment geology. Snapping turtles patrol quiet eddies. Beavers engineer along calmer tributaries. River otters slip between rock and current.

The geological backbone of this ecosystem is the Niagara Escarpment, recognized as a UNESCO World Biosphere Reserve. Its ancient forests cling to limestone and shale layers exposed over millennia. These forests provide habitat for specialized species found nowhere else in such concentration.

Yet this vitality faces pressure

Invasive species such as the Emerald Ash Borer and Hemlock Woolly Adelgid threaten native trees. Phragmites crowd wetlands. Shoreline modifications and hydropower diversions have altered habitat patterns. Conservation efforts now include bioengineering techniques to stabilize erosion, habitat restoration, and active protection of species like the bald eagle and peregrine falcon.

Sacred Corridor

Long before the river was measured in megawatts, it was measured in meaning.

The Niagara corridor sits within the traditional homelands of the Haudenosaunee Confederacy, a political and cultural alliance that shaped the northeastern woodlands for centuries before European arrival. To reduce this place to scenery is to misunderstand it. The river was not backdrop. It was participant.

Waterways were the highways of the continent. The Niagara River linked Lake Erie to Lake Ontario, and through them to a vast inland sea of travel and exchange. Canoes moved furs, corn, stories, diplomacy. The Falls themselves interrupted navigation, but they did not sever connection. Portage paths wrapped around the cataract, worn smooth by generations of foot traffic carrying goods and memory.

The gorge was not an obstacle. It was a hinge.

The nations of the Confederacy, including the Seneca, Cayuga, Onondaga, Oneida, Mohawk, and later the Tuscarora, understood the river as part of a living system. The Seneca, whose western territories encompassed the Niagara region, acted as Keepers of the Western Door. The phrase was not poetic flourish. It was responsibility. Borders were not lines drawn on paper but zones of relationship.

The Falls held spiritual significance. The constant thunder suggested presence. The mist rising from the plunge basin blurred the boundary between solid and vapor, carth and sky. Oral traditions speak of beings and forces inhabiting powerful natural sites. Whether told as legend or teaching, the stories anchored the Falls within a cosmology where land and water possessed agency.

European explorers would later write of the spectacle in tones of astonishment. They were witnessing something that had long been known.

Trade networks radiated outward from this corridor. Before colonial forts appeared, Indigenous diplomacy governed passage. Alliances shifted. Conflicts arose. Yet the river remained a central artery in regional politics. Control of portage routes meant influence over commerce.

When French missionaries and traders entered the region in the seventeenth century, they

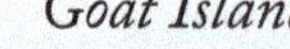
Goat Island

encountered a landscape already structured by Indigenous governance. They recorded impressions of the Falls, sometimes exaggerating their scale for audiences abroad. But their presence marked a turning point. The river that had connected communities would become a contested imperial boundary.

The word "Niagara" itself likely derives from Indigenous language, often interpreted as "thundering waters" or "neck." The dual translation is fitting. The river narrows. It roars. It compresses vast flow into a dramatic descent. Language preserved the sensory truth of the place.

Daily life along the corridor followed seasonal rhythms. Fishing camps formed where currents allowed. Fields were planted in fertile soils left by retreating glaciers. Forests supplied timber and game. The gorge offered both protection and challenge. Children would have known its trails intimately, the sound of rapids as familiar as wind in leaves.

Then came treaties.

As colonial powers vied for dominance in North America, alliances with the Haudenosaunee Confederacy became strategic necessity. Diplomacy was conducted through councils and wampum belts, each bead a mnemonic device encoding agreements. Yet the balance of power shifted with European settlement density and military force.

By the late eighteenth century, after the American Revolution, land cessions accelerated. The Treaty of Canandaigua in 1794 recognized certain Haudenosaunee lands, but pressure for expansion continued. The Niagara frontier became a site of layered sovereignty: Indigenous, British, American.

The river began to transform from corridor to boundary.

Still, Indigenous presence did not vanish. Communities endured displacement, negotiated survival, maintained cultural continuity. The Seneca Nation of Indians retains territory within western New York, including lands not far from the Falls. Sovereignty is not an artifact of the past here. It is a present-tense reality.

Modern visitors standing at the brink often encounter plaques and interpretive signs acknowledging Indigenous history. The recognition is necessary, but it is not sufficient. The deeper story is not simply that Indigenous people were here first. It is that the conceptual framework for understanding this landscape began with them.

To view the Falls solely as commodity or attraction is a relatively recent habit.

For centuries, the Niagara corridor functioned as connective tissue in a vast network of trade and diplomacy. The portage path that once carried bundles of fur would later carry artillery during wartime, then rails and tourists. The function changed. The geography did not.

The sacred and the strategic coexisted here.

As settlement intensified in the nineteenth century, Indigenous communities faced marginalization and removal from lands that had structured their identity. Yet cultural memory remained anchored to place. Ceremonies continued. Oral histories persisted. The sound of the water did not change allegiance.

Niagara Falls, New York would eventually rise as a city defined by industry and tourism. But beneath that civic identity lies an older understanding of the corridor as relational space, where water binds rather than divides.

The river still connects four Great Lakes before plunging over stone. It still moves with a force that predates property deeds. To write its history responsibly is to begin not with fences or factories, but with the people who first recognized that this was not merely a waterfall.

It was a living threshold.

Naming the Wonder

The first Europeans who saw Niagara Falls did not discover it. They translated it.

In the seventeenth century, French missionaries and explorers pushed deeper into the interior of North America, following waterways that Indigenous nations had traveled for generations. Among them was Louis Hennepin, a Recollect friar whose 1678 expedition brought him to the cataract.

Hennepin's published account of the Falls in 1683 carried the thunder across the Atlantic. His engravings portrayed a towering cascade, exaggerated in height but accurate in drama. Readers in Europe encountered Niagara not as geography but as spectacle. The Falls entered the Western imagination as sublime force, a New World marvel worthy of awe and imperial ambition.

It was a beginning of sorts, though not the first telling.

The act of naming has weight. The word "Niagara," drawn from Indigenous language, survived in French spelling and later English usage. But with publication came framing. The Falls were described as wild, untamed, magnificent. The adjectives carried implication. What was powerful could also be possessed.

Exploration in this era was rarely neutral. Rivers were routes to trade. Trade was pathway to empire. The Niagara corridor, linking inland lakes to the St. Lawrence River, held strategic importance beyond its scenic drama. Control of this passage meant influence over commerce and movement.

French interests established a presence along the river. Mission outposts and trading posts appeared. Alliances with Indigenous nations were cultivated and strained. The Falls, though not directly navigable, became part of a larger network of imperial calculation.

Maps began to circulate.

Cartographers sketched the Great Lakes with increasing accuracy. The Niagara River and its cataract were marked as landmark and obstacle. The gorge appeared as incision in the land. What had been known intimately through lived experience was now abstracted onto parchment.

Yet for all the mapping, the Falls resisted containment. They could be drawn but not quieted. Travelers described the ground trembling beneath their feet. Mist rose like weather. Sound swallowed speech.

By the eighteenth century, Niagara was firmly embedded in European travel literature. Writers compared it to Alpine landscapes and biblical imagery. The language leaned toward the sublime, that aesthetic category describing beauty edged with terror. Standing at the brink was framed as moral experience, confrontation with power beyond human scale.

The rhetoric elevated the Falls while subtly shifting their meaning. They became emblem of the New World itself: vast, dramatic, waiting to be interpreted.

As British control replaced French dominance following the Seven Years' War, the Niagara frontier took on additional political tension. Fortifications strengthened. Trade patterns shifted. The river corridor became contested space between empires. The Falls remained constant, indifferent to flag changes.

Above: Portrait of Louis Hennepin, 1694

Niagara Falls by Father Louis Hennepin, 1698

The late eighteenth and early nineteenth centuries introduced a new layer: tourism.

Improved roads and steamboat routes made the journey to Niagara more accessible. Visitors recorded impressions in diaries. Artists sketched panoramas. Engravings circulated widely. The Falls were marketed as destination. A sense of pilgrimage developed, especially among Americans seeking symbols of national grandeur distinct from Europe's ruins and cathedrals.

Honeymoon travel to Niagara Falls began in the early nineteenth century and accelerated with rail expansion. The association of the Falls with romance grew from a mixture of marketing and mythology. The thunderous backdrop lent emotional intensity to private vows.

But commercialization brought friction.

Private landowners fenced off vantage points and charged admission. Visitors complained of aggressive vendors and obstructed views. The tension between profit and access surfaced repeatedly. The question emerged: Could wonder be owned?

By the mid-nineteenth century, reformers argued that the Falls were too significant to be fragmented by speculation. The "Free Niagara" movement sought to preserve public access and curb unchecked development. Their efforts eventually led to the establishment of Niagara Falls State Park in 1885, the first state park in

Thomas Hart Benton, Niagara, 1961

Commissioned in 1958 by Robert Moses for the New York State Power Authority and installed in 1961 at Power Vista, the visitor center of the Robert Moses Niagara Power Plant.

After a year and a half of research and six months of painting, Thomas Hart Benton (1889–1975), then regarded as America's foremost muralist, completed this sweeping work. The mural dramatizes Father Louis Hennepin, Franciscan chaplain to La Salle's expedition, standing before the thunder of Niagara Falls. Though not the first European to see the cataract, Hennepin was the first to describe it for a global audience, transforming spectacle into story and setting Niagara on the world's stage.

the United States.

Naming had evolved into stewardship.

Throughout this period, the Falls functioned as mirror. Artists projected emotion onto the torrent. Writers used it as metaphor for divine power, democratic potential, or industrial promise. Politicians referenced it in speeches as symbol of American vigor.

Yet beneath the language, the geology persisted in its steady retreat upstream.

By the end of the nineteenth century, another naming was underway. The Falls were no longer described solely as sublime spectacle. They were being described in technical terms: cubic feet per second, hydraulic head, horsepower. Engineers saw in the cataract a system waiting to be optimized.

The transition from wonder to resource did not erase awe. It layered it.

Niagara Falls, New York grew alongside this evolving perception. The city emerged not only because the waterfall was beautiful, but because it was useful. The language surrounding it shifted from poetry to power output.

Still, even as turbines would soon redirect part of the flow, the original naming endured. Travelers continued to write of mist and rainbows. The roar remained theatrical. The Falls resisted reduction to single identity.

They were at once sacred corridor, imperial landmark, tourist destination, and industrial opportunity.

To name the wonder was to begin a long conversation about ownership, access, and purpose. Each era supplied its vocabulary. The water supplied continuity.

Niagara Falls was never silent. The only question was how it would be described, and by whom.

War on the Water

The river that carried trade could also carry troops.

By the early nineteenth century, the Niagara corridor had shifted from imperial curiosity to strategic fault line. The American Revolution had redrawn allegiances, but it had not quieted tension along the border. The Niagara River became a dividing seam between the United States and British-controlled Upper Canada. Water does not recognize borders. Armies do.

At the mouth of the river stood Old Fort Niagara, a stone sentinel whose walls had already flown French and British flags before becoming American. Its position commanded access between Lake Ontario and the interior. Whoever controlled this gateway could regulate movement of men and material.

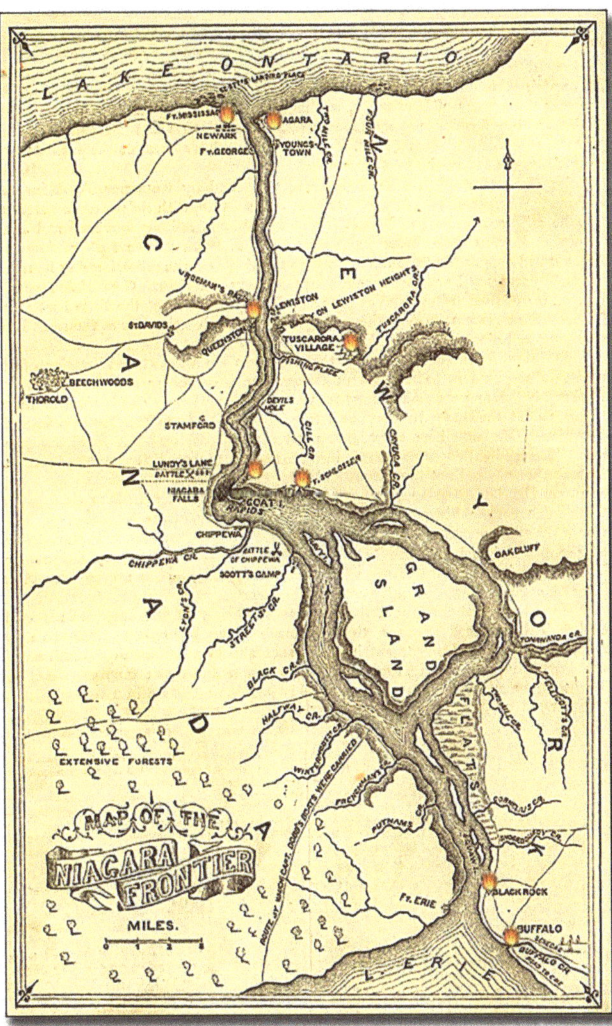

When the War of 1812 erupted, the Niagara frontier ignited quickly.

The conflict was not fought in distant capitals. It unfolded in farm fields, along riverbanks, and in villages that had only recently begun to stabilize. Skirmishes flared along the water. Artillery echoed through the gorge. The Falls, indifferent as ever, continued their descent while cannon smoke drifted through mist.

The river both separated and entangled communities. Families had kin on opposite shores. Commerce had flowed freely before hostilities. Now crossings became tactical maneuvers. Winter ice could create temporary bridges, altering defensive calculations overnight.

One of the defining episodes on the American side was the burning of Buffalo in December 1813. British forces and their Indigenous allies crossed the river after American troops had torched the Canadian village of Newark. Retaliation was swift. Buffalo and nearby settlements were set ablaze. Structures that had taken years to erect were reduced to ash in hours.

Niagara Falls, then little more than scattered settlement near the cataract, absorbed the shock of proximity. The frontier was not abstract policy. It was vulnerability.

Rebuilding became reflex.

Homes rose again. Fields were replanted. The war concluded in 1815 with the Treaty of Ghent, restoring boundaries largely to their prewar lines. The river resumed its quieter traffic. Yet memory lingered. The Niagara frontier had proven how quickly a scenic corridor could become battleground.

Queenston Heights battle re-enactment

The conflict reshaped the psychology of the region. Living beside an international boundary required vigilance. Fortifications were strengthened. Militia traditions persisted. The landscape itself bore marks of conflict, from earthworks to cemeteries.

Over time, the border softened.

The nineteenth century saw increasing cross-border cooperation even as national identities hardened elsewhere. Trade resumed. Ferries connected communities. Later, bridges would formalize the link. But the War of 1812 remained embedded in local consciousness as a reminder that geography carries consequence.

The Niagara River's narrowness in places made it both bridge and barrier. It compressed space. One could see the opposite shore clearly. Distance was visible but deceptive. The ease of view did not guarantee ease of passage.

The Falls themselves offered no military advantage in the conventional sense. They were too unruly to harness for defense. Yet their presence shaped strategy. Portage routes around the cataract were vital. Control of those routes meant control of inland access.

As decades passed, the frontier transformed from flashpoint to framework. The border settled into administrative reality. Customs houses replaced cannon batteries. Diplomacy replaced siege.

But the imprint of war did not vanish entirely. It influenced infrastructure decisions, settlement patterns, and civic identity. Niagara Falls grew with an awareness of its edge condition. It was a city that faced outward as much as inward.

The river that once carried soldiers would soon carry tourists in greater numbers. The same water that reflected flames in 1813 would later reflect electric illumination. Conflict yielded to commerce. Yet the lesson endured: proximity to power, whether natural or political, demands resilience.

The Niagara frontier had burned. It rebuilt.

The water kept moving.

Fort Schlosser

Portage, Power, and the Old Stone Chimney

Before turbines harnessed the current and steel bridges leapt the gorge, the upper Niagara River was a military corridor. Control the portage, and you controlled the passage between Lake Erie and Lake Ontario.

Fort Schlosser stood near present-day Niagara Falls, just above the American Rapids, guarding the upper landing where goods were unloaded before being hauled around the Falls. It was part of a chain of frontier defenses that stitched the river into empire.

The geography dictated the strategy. The Falls blocked navigation. Cargo and military supplies had to be carried overland along the portage road, then reloaded downstream. At the lower end of that route, Fort Grey guarded Lewiston. At the river's mouth, Fort Niagara commanded the entrance to Lake Ontario. Together, these posts formed a defensive spine along the Niagara corridor.

The story begins in the mid-eighteenth century. The French, intent on securing their Great Lakes network, fortified the upper landing prior to the French and Indian War. When British forces advanced in 1759, threatening Fort Niagara, the French made a stark calculation. Rather than allow their upper post to fall intact into British hands, they burned it themselves before marching north to reinforce Fort Niagara. The river, already loud, absorbed another kind of violence: fire as strategy.

After the British captured Fort Niagara, they consolidated control of the corridor. Around 1760, they established Fort Schlosser, named for

Fort Schlosser

Old Stone Chimney

Captain Johann Schlosser, a British officer killed during the campaign. The fort incorporated the Old Stone Chimney from nearby Fort Little Niagara, a surviving fragment of earlier French occupation. That chimney became both architectural anchor and symbol of layered control: French foundation, British fortification, later American inheritance.

Fort Schlosser was not massive. It was practical. A supply depot. A checkpoint. A guard over movement. Its significance lay less in dramatic battle and more in logistics. Armies move on provisions; provisions moved along the portage.

Following the American Revolution, British forces lingered along the frontier until the Jay Treaty of 1796 compelled withdrawal. The fort passed into American hands. During the War of 1812, the Niagara corridor again became contested ground. Troops and supplies passed through the upper landing. The river resumed its role as border and battleground.

By the mid-nineteenth century, military urgency faded. Tourism and commerce replaced redcoats and muskets. The wooden stockade disappeared. The Old Stone Chimney endured as a relic. The remains is the Old Stone Chimney was moved to the former Porter Park near the intersection of Buffalo Avenue and the Robert Moses Parkway in 1957 to near a traffic circle about 1.5 miles from the original fort site.

Fort Schlosser reminds us that long before Niagara was spectacle or industry, it was strategy. The water determined everything.

It still does.

Channeling the Current

The Niagara Falls Hydraulic Canal

Before alternating current lit distant cities, before massive underground tunnels redirected billions of gallons each day, Niagara Falls harnessed its power the direct way: with a shovel, a surveyor's chain, and stubborn ambition.

The Niagara Falls Hydraulic Canal was one of the earliest large-scale attempts to convert the Falls from spectacle into sustained industrial force. It marked the moment when admiration yielded to application.

The idea took shape in the 1850s. Entrepreneurs such as Augustus Porter and other local investors understood what the geography offered. The Niagara River, fed by four Great Lakes, delivered an immense, continuous flow just above the brink. If even a fraction of that water could be diverted inland and dropped through a controlled descent, it could turn wheels, spin shafts, and power machinery far more reliably than steam engines.

Construction of the canal began in 1853 under the Niagara Falls Hydraulic Company. Workers carved a channel from the upper river, running roughly parallel to its natural course before directing water through vertical penstocks to mills below. The engineering was ambitious for its time. The canal stretched nearly a mile and was designed to feed multiple industrial sites along Buffalo Avenue.

Water entered quietly. It exited with purpose.

The system allowed factories to be positioned inland rather than clinging precariously to the immediate riverbank. That mattered. Direct waterwheels at the edge of the river were vulnerable to ice, fluctuation, and erosion. The canal created a semi-controlled grid. It separated the point of diversion from the point of use.

By the late 1850s and 1860s, mills and manufacturing plants began clustering along the canal corridor. Flour mills, paper producers, and machine shops capitalized on the steady mechanical energy. The roar of the Falls was joined by the clatter of belts and gears. Niagara Falls was becoming more than a tourist stop. It was becoming an industrial town.

The Hydraulic Canal transformed

Milling District

local economics. Cheap waterpower attracted capital. Capital attracted labor. Brick factory buildings rose along Buffalo Avenue, their windows tall to capture light for work floors driven by canal-fed turbines. The canal became an industrial spine, shaping the city's growth pattern.

It was not yet electricity. It was torque.

But innovation rarely leaps in a single bound. The canal established precedent. It demonstrated that Niagara's force could be channeled, measured, sold. Engineers observing its operation began imagining larger systems. By the 1880s and 1890s, technological advances in electrical generation made it possible to convert falling water into current transmitted miles away.

The Adams Power Plant, completed in 1895, would eclipse the Hydraulic Canal in scale and influence. Its underground tunnels and alternating current generators powered Buffalo and beyond. But that achievement stood on the canal's shoulders. The earlier system had already proven that industrial infrastructure could coexist with the Falls without diminishing its visual drama.

The canal also had limitations. Water levels fluctuated seasonally. Ice remained a threat. And as industry intensified in the late nineteenth and early twentieth centuries, demand for power outstripped what the original canal system could reliably supply. Larger, more sophisticated hydroelectric facilities gradually replaced mechanical waterpower.

Over time, sections of the Hydraulic Canal fell into disuse. Some stretches were filled. Others were absorbed into evolving industrial parcels. Yet its imprint remains etched into the geography of Buffalo Avenue and the city's industrial layout.

The Hydraulic Canal represents a hinge in Niagara's story.

Before it, the Falls were primarily a destination. After it, they were also a resource.

The canal altered the psychology of the place. The water still fell in awe-inspiring sheets over limestone ledges. But now, inland, it worked in measured increments. It turned productivity into profit. It shifted Niagara Falls from scenic margin to manufacturing hub.

There is an irony embedded in its history. The canal sought to domesticate a fraction of the river's energy, yet it depended entirely on the continuity of the greater system. Without the Great Lakes feeding the Niagara River, without gravity pulling water toward Lake Ontario, there would be nothing to divert.

The Hydraulic Canal did not tame Niagara.

It negotiated with it.

And in that negotiation lay the blueprint for everything that followed: the power plants, the factories, the skyline of brick and steel. The canal was rehearsal before the grand performance of hydroelectric modernity.

The water still falls.

But in the 1850s, it also began to turn the city.

The Public Claim

By the middle of the nineteenth century, Niagara Falls had become a destination in the modern sense of the word.

Rail lines stitched the cataract to New York City, Boston, Philadelphia. Steamships carried visitors across the Great Lakes. Guidebooks printed schedules and recommendations. Honeymooners arrived with trunks and expectation. The Falls were no longer rumor carried by engraving. They were itinerary.

And where visitors gather, commerce follows.

Niagara Falls in the 1800s was an industrialist's dreamland and a huckster's paradise. Cheap waterpower abounded, all you had to do was scratch a channel, divert a small portion of the mighty Niagara past your mill, and you were in business. The river did the labor. You collected the reward. Just as easily, an enterprising "entrepreneur" could buy a small parcel of land with a view, erect a tall fence, and charge visitors from far and wide exorbitant fees to get a glimpse of the thunderous cataract. The Eighth Wonder of the World, once you paid enough to see it.

Hotels multiplied along the American side. Viewing platforms extended outward like mechanical balconies. Entrepreneurs fenced off pathways and charged admission to stand at the brink. Vendors sold souvenirs, snacks, vantage points. The sublime acquired a ticket booth.

Many travelers complained.

They had come seeking transcendence and encountered turnstiles. They had expected grandeur and found aggressive solicitation. Writers described the irritation of paying repeatedly for access to what felt elemental and universal. The tension was not simply aesthetic. It was philosophical.

Could a waterfall be owned?

By the 1860s, the land surrounding the American Falls was largely in private hands. Industrial speculation and tourism development had carved the landscape into parcels, each one a small kingdom with a fence line and a fee. The river roared freely, but the ground beneath

Above: Friends Henry Hobson Richardson, William Dorsheimer, and Frederick Law Olmsted (Simulation)

visitors' feet did not. Even the act of looking became transactional: a coin for the best sightline, another for a walkway, another for the privilege of standing where the light and mist aligned.

Niagara, meanwhile, was beginning to do what famous places always do. It pulled in the world, and the world tried to leave fingerprints on it. The American side grew busy in a particular nineteenth-century way: ambitious, improvised, slightly predatory. It was not merely that commerce existed, but that it crowded the experience. "Hucksters" became shorthand for the men who stepped into a visitor's path with rehearsed urgency, selling trinkets, photos, "best views," and sometimes just the illusion of access. If the Falls were a cathedral, too many people were selling pews.

A reform movement began to take shape. Known as the "Free Niagara" movement, it drew support from artists, writers, and civic leaders who believed the Falls represented more than private opportunity. The cause gained momentum from a simple premise: Niagara's grandeur was a public asset, and public assets should not be subdivided into tollbooths.

Enter Frederick Law Olmsted, the landscape architect who had made his name designing Central Park in New York City and leading the effort to conserve the Yosemite Valley in California. In August 1869, Olmsted was working on the Buffalo parks and parkway system when he took time out to visit Niagara Falls.

He rented a room at the famous hotel by the American Falls, the sprawling Cataract House, the kind of place where the lobby carried the scent of cigars, wet wool, and money in motion.

Opposite: From Terrifying myths and History Reel -https://www.facebook.com/TerrifyingMyths/reels/

There he was joined by William Dorsheimer, the district attorney for northern New York and the man who headed the Buffalo parkways commission. Also at the hotel was a young, not-yet-famous architect, Henry Hobson Richardson, who was designing Dorsheimer's mansion on Delaware Avenue.

On August 8, the three friends took a stroll on Goat Island, pretty much the last piece of unspoiled land at the Falls. Like others before them, they were appalled at how much this marvel of nature had been obscured from view. High fences cut through sightlines like bad punctuation. Mills and factories pressed along the gorge, not content to borrow the river's energy, but eager to crowd it, claim it, market it, and monetize every angle of it.

The next day they convened a meeting in

Frederic Edwin Church's Niagara. From the National Gallery of Art.

Dorsheimer's hotel room. That detail matters. Niagara's liberation began not with a grand public ceremony, but with men sitting in a private room, deciding that the arrangement was intolerable. They were joined by other prominent figures who shared a vision of a Niagara free of obstruction, where visitors could gaze upon the rushing waters and ramble through wooded pathways to their hearts' content. Thus began a long campaign: the Free Niagara movement.

Olmsted's argument was not sentimental. It was structural. The Falls did not need ornament. They needed relief. The campaign emphasized restraint rather than embellishment. The Falls did not need grand staircases or ornate pavilions. They needed clearing of obstructions. They needed space. The design philosophy favored naturalistic paths, open sightlines, and minimal

intrusion between visitor and water.

This was a radical idea in an era that loved decoration. It asked for humility, and humility is rarely profitable.

But the movement had allies, and not subtle ones.

Over the next decade and more, Free Niagara conservationists brought to bear the influence of some of the continent's most famous and influential figures. Olmsted and his partner Calvert Vaux were joined by voices that carried cultural weight: the novelist Henry James; the Governor General of Canada, Lord Dufferin; William Morris, founder of the Arts and Crafts movement; intellectuals and writers including Ralph Waldo Emerson, Henry Wadsworth Longfellow, Thomas Carlyle, John Ruskin, and Charles Darwin. Their support signaled something essential: Niagara was not merely local property. It was a landmark of global stature, and its degradation was a public embarrassment.

The painter Frederic Edwin Church supplied the movement with an image powerful enough to do what speeches sometimes cannot. His vast 1857 panorama, Niagara, drew crowds on international tours and made the Falls' precarious condition visible to people who had never stood at the brink. In New York City, viewers paid to see Niagara on canvas, which only sharpened the irony: the real Niagara was being fenced off and sold in fragments.

A picture can be propaganda when the truth is on its side.

For more than a dozen years the Free Niagara conservationists lobbied the governments of New York State and Ontario. They wrote reports, hosted meetings, organized pressure, and refused to accept the idea that the nation's most famous waterfall should be experienced through gaps in fences.

Finally, in 1883 came the breakthrough.

Dorsheimer's Buffalo friend Grover Cleveland became governor of New York. Politics is often less about persuasion than about proximity, and the movement now had access to power that could translate ideals into law. Cleveland signed a bill calling for the establishment of a state park at Niagara.

Two years later, in 1885, New York State acted in full.

The Niagara Reservation became reality, the first state park anywhere in the United States. Land was acquired through state funding and legal mechanisms that curtailed private control of prime viewing areas. Fences came down. Vantage points reopened. The decision was precedent-setting. It framed preservation not as luxury but as civic obligation. The Falls were declared a public trust.

Across the river, Ontario followed with its own vision. In 1888, Queen Victoria Park opened on the Canadian side. Where New York's park leaned toward pastoral naturalism, Ontario's design reflected a more formal English garden sensibility. Different aesthetics, shared purpose: remove the clutter, reclaim the view, restore dignity to the landscape.

Both are surpassingly beautiful.

On the U.S. side, commissioners began clearing out structures that blocked the views along the upper rapids, limiting factories to areas downstream from the Falls. It was not an abolition of commerce, but a boundary: industry would not squat on the spectacle itself. Soon Olmsted and Vaux began the landscaping that gives the American side its character today, ambling walkways, wooded glades, and open greens where visitors can contemplate the beauty of nature without a billboard elbowing

View from Prospect Point -1902

into the frame.

The transformation did not eliminate commerce. Hotels and attractions remained integral to the city's economy. But a line had been drawn. The brink itself would not become carnival.

Tourism continued to expand.

By the late nineteenth century, Niagara Falls was firmly embedded in the cultural imagination as honeymoon capital. Newlyweds posed for photographs in formal dress, mist rising behind them like theatrical backdrop. The ritual of visiting the Falls became almost obligatory among certain classes. Romance fused with geography, and the Falls became shorthand for beginnings.

At the same time, technological spectacle began to layer atop natural drama. Tightrope walkers drew crowds. Illumination experiments in the late nineteenth century bathed the water in colored light. Niagara was not only preserved. It was staged. The park created a buffer, but it could not halt evolution. It could only insist that evolution answer to stewardship.

And just beyond that buffer, as the twentieth century approached, another appetite grew.

Industrial ambitions gathered strength along the river corridor. Hydropower facilities would soon divert substantial portions of the Niagara's flow. The preservation of scenic frontage would coexist uneasily with the harnessing of energy out of sight. Niagara would become both shrine and engine.

Yet the creation of the park ensured something crucial. It guaranteed that the public would retain access to the elemental experience: standing at the edge, feeling the tremor underfoot, watching water fold into mist.

The Public Claim was not simply about land. It was about philosophy. It asserted that certain landscapes possess collective value beyond immediate profit. It argued that wonder should not be rationed.

Niagara Falls became both attraction and inheritance.

Visitors still arrive in waves, cameras lifted, ponchos snapping in the wind. They move along paths envisioned more than a century ago, largely unaware of the debates that secured their footing. They see the water. They may not see the argument that made the view possible.

But the argument is still there, embedded in every unobstructed sightline.

The Falls do not need advocacy. They generate awe without assistance.

But the land around them required decision.

It all could have turned out quite differently at Niagara, had it not been for that Goat Island stroll Frederick Law Olmsted and his two friends took back in August 1869. In that walk is the hinge of Niagara's public future: the moment when enough people decided the world's most famous waterfall should not be a fenced commodity, but a shared experience.

The roar continues. The access remains.

And every time someone stands at the railing for free, letting the mist settle on their sleeves without paying a stranger for permission, they are living inside the victory of a nineteenth-century idea: that power, whether natural or industrial, demands stewardship.

Stand at Terrapin Point today and you are standing on altered ground.

The Island Between the Falls

Goat Island

Stand on Goat Island and the Niagara River surrounds you like a living engine of water. To one side, the American and Bridal Veil Falls tumble toward the gorge. To the other, the river bends toward the thunderous curve of the Horseshoe Falls. Today the island is a peaceful part of Niagara Falls State Park, but its history is far older, stranger, and more dramatic than the calm walking paths might suggest.

Long before bridges carried tourists across the river, the island was known as Iris Island, named after the Greek goddess of the rainbow. Mist from the Falls constantly fills the air here, and rainbows often appear in the sunlight, giving the name a poetic logic. But history had other plans for the island's identity.

The story of Goat Island begins in the eighteenth century with a man named John Stedman. Stedman had lived through one of the most violent moments in early Niagara history. In 1763, he survived the Devil's Hole Massacre, when Seneca warriors attacked a British supply convoy traveling along the Niagara Gorge. Eighty soldiers and civilians were killed. Stedman was one of only two survivors.

Afterward, Stedman continued working along the Niagara Portage. British Superintendent Sir William Johnson had appointed him "Master of

Goat Island Toll Booth

the Portage," responsible for overseeing the difficult task of transporting goods around Niagara Falls along the steep escarpment route between Lake Ontario and Lake Erie.

In 1764, peace negotiations between the British and the Seneca resulted in the transfer of land along the Niagara River to British control. According to later accounts, Stedman claimed that the Seneca granted him the islands above the Falls during these talks. Whether by formal grant or personal claim, Stedman eventually took possession of the island.

During the 1770s, Stedman transported a small herd of goats to the island. The plan was practical. Wolves roamed the mainland forests, and the island seemed like a safe refuge for the animals. But Niagara winters can be merciless. During the brutal winter of 1780, nearly all of the goats perished in the cold. Only one survived.

The story lingered, and the island soon became known as Goat Island.

Stedman eventually left the Niagara frontier in 1795, placing his land under the care of a friend. By 1801, the State of New York took possession of the property, including the island. For a time, the island remained mostly wild. Bears, wolves, and deer were common sightings in the forests near the roaring river.

A new chapter began in 1816 when General Augustus Porter, a prominent landowner and U.S. commissioner, purchased Goat Island from the state. Porter quickly recognized its potential as a tourist destination.

In 1817, he built the first wooden bridge connecting the mainland to the island. The Niagara River, however, is never easily controlled. Ice destroyed the bridge the following winter. Undeterred, Porter built another bridge in 1818, this time closer to the Falls. Visitors could now reach the island and walk along the edges of one of the world's great natural spectacles.

As tourism grew, the island became a center of viewing platforms and attractions. One of the most controversial was the Terrapin Tower, built by the Porter family in 1833 near the brink of Horseshoe Falls. Rising about 45 feet, the stone tower allowed visitors to climb above the edge of the Falls for a dramatic view of the rushing water below. Some admired it. Others believed it spoiled the natural beauty of the landscape. In 1873, the tower was demolished.

During the nineteenth century, Goat Island also

Opposite: Goat Island

P.T. Barnum and General Tom Thumb

became the focus of preservation debates. Industrial development along the Niagara River threatened to transform the area surrounding the Falls into a landscape of mills, canals, and power works. One particularly unusual proposal came from the famous showman P. T. Barnum.

Barnum envisioned purchasing Goat Island and turning it into a year-round spectacle. His plan reportedly included fencing off the island and charging admission, possibly even hosting circus attractions beside the Falls. Fortunately for the scenery, the plan never materialized.

Public concern about protecting Niagara's natural beauty eventually led to action. In 1885, New York State established the Niagara Reservation, the first state park in the United States. Goat Island became a central part of the protected landscape.

Today, the island remains the heart of the park. Visitors walk its wooded trails to reach Terrapin Point, where the Horseshoe Falls curve into Canada. At the base of the cliffs lies the famous Cave of the Winds, where wooden walkways bring visitors close enough to feel the power of Bridal Veil Falls.

From Goat Island, footbridges also lead to the Three Sisters Islands, named for Asenath, Angeline, and Celinda Eliza Whitney, daughters of early Niagara hotel owner General Parkhurst Whitney. The sisters reportedly crossed to the islands in 1816 during a winter ice jam, becoming the first recorded visitors there. The small islands, once called the Moss Islands, now provide some of the closest views of the raging upper Niagara River rapids.

Through wars, entrepreneurs, and grand schemes, Goat Island has endured. Surrounded by thunder and mist, it remains what early visitors first

Goat Island Hill - 1902

At the Edge

Terrapin Tower and the Making of Terrapin Point

The wind comes hard off the Horseshoe Falls. The water curves in a vast green arc before breaking into white violence below. It feels elemental, permanent.

It is not.

Terrapin Point, located at the western tip of Goat Island, was once something smaller and stranger: a cluster of rocks at the very brink of the Horseshoe Falls known as the Terrapin Rocks. They earned the name because their rounded forms resembled giant tortoises sunning themselves at the edge of catastrophe.

In the early nineteenth century, those rocks were disconnected from Goat Island.

In 1817, Peter and Augustus Porter built a 300-foot timber walkway from Goat Island to what was then called Porter's Bluff. The heavy plank structure extended outward to within ten feet of the crest line of the Falls. It was audacious. Visitors could stand over the drop, suspended above thunder.

A few steps below the bluff lay the Terrapin Rocks themselves. The location carried deeper meaning. It was believed to be a site where Native American warriors once cast offerings into the river for the Great Spirit of Niagara. The brink was never just geology. It was ceremony.

In 1829, on those rocks, General Parkhurst Whitney constructed what became known as Terrapin Tower, the first observation tower at Niagara Falls. The structure was modest but bold: a circular, lighthouse-like tower estimated between 30 and 45 feet tall and about 12 feet in diameter. Inside, a spiral staircase led to a viewing platform.

Visitors climbed for perspective.

Some praised the proximity. Others argued the tower disturbed the natural beauty of the Falls. Francis Abbott, an early showman, reportedly performed acrobatic feats at the edge of the walkway, blurring spectacle and risk.

In 1872, Terrapin Tower was purposely blown apart, not because it had become unsafe, but rather not to compete with a new tower at Prospect Park. Those plans for a new tower were never acted upon and a replacement tower was never built.

The timber walkway remained for decades. In the early twentieth century, it was replaced by a steel catwalk leading to the rocks and the brink.

Then in 1954, Terrapin Rocks were de-watered. The catwalk was removed. The area was backfilled to create the broad viewing plaza known today as Terrapin Point. The reshaping was partly aesthetic, partly hydraulic. Rockfalls near the crest and upstream water diversion for hydroelectric generation had created irregular flow patterns. Reengineering the brink restored symmetry.

What was once a precarious outcrop became a stable platform.

Terrapin Tower is gone. The rocks are buried. The walkway survives only in photographs.

But the location remains what it has always been: the closest legal place to stand beside the Horseshoe Falls on the American side.

At the edge.

Where people have always wanted to go

There are two ways to approach a waterfall.

You can lean back from the railing and let the

Opposite: Terrapin Tower -1830

Risk & Reputation

mist settle on your coat.

Or you can climb into a barrel.

Niagara Falls has always attracted both kinds of people.

By the mid-nineteenth century, the cataract was no longer merely scenic. It was theatrical. Railroads delivered audiences by the thousands. Hotels filled. Newspapers amplified every unusual event. The Falls had become a stage without curtains.

In 1859, the French tightrope walker Jean François "Blondin" Gravelet *(left)* stretched a cable across the gorge and stepped into open air. Crowds gathered along the banks, straining for view. Blondin crossed not once but repeatedly, sometimes blindfolded, sometimes pushing a wheelbarrow, once carrying his manager on his back. The act was absurd and astonishing in equal measure. The Falls, once framed as divine force, now hosted spectacle.

Risk became currency.

The nineteenth century was an age of public daring. Balloon ascents. Railroad stunts. Feats of endurance that blurred the line between bravery and self-promotion. Niagara offered a ready-made proving ground. Its scale guaranteed drama. Survival guaranteed fame.

The "Barrel Brigade" entered folklore in 1901.

On October 24 of that year, a 63-year-old Michigan schoolteacher named Annie Edson Taylor climbed into a custom-made wooden barrel padded with a mattress. She was a widow with limited means. She saw the plunge as investment. The descent took minutes. The preparation had taken months. The barrel vanished over the brink and into mist.

When it was recovered downstream, battered but intact, Taylor emerged shaken but alive. She had become the first known person to survive a deliberate trip over the Falls. Fame followed. Wealth did not. Promoters profited more reliably than performers. Taylor spent years selling souvenirs and photographs, her legend outpacing her bank account.

Others followed her example.

In 1911, Bobby Leach rode over the Horseshoe Falls in a crude steel barrel braking both kneecaps and his jaw. Years later, he slipped on an orange peel and died from complications due to gangrene. In 1930, George Stathakis rode a one-ton wooden barrel over the brink. His barrel lodged behind the curtain of water for fourteen hours. He carried only enough air for three. He died. His 105-year-old turtle survived.

Opposite: 1920 -Englishman Charles G. Stephens and his wooden barrel.

Bobby Leach

The Falls did not answer the question of bravery versus folly.

Municipal authorities struggled to respond. Public fascination translated into tourism revenue. Yet each attempt carried risk not only to the daredevil but to rescuers and bystanders. Over time, regulations tightened. Permits became mandatory. Unauthorized stunts resulted in fines and prosecution on both sides of the border.

Still, the myth persisted.

In 1960, seven-year-old Roger Woodward survived an accidental plunge over the Horseshoe Falls after a boating mishap. The event was labeled a miracle. In 1984, Canadian Karel Soucek successfully rode a barrel over the Falls, only to die the following year attempting to recreate the stunt indoors in Houston. In 1995, Steven Trotter and Lori Martin became one of several two-person teams to survive the drop. Others were less fortunate. Jesse Sharp, who paddled over the Falls in a kayak in 1990 without a life vest, was never recovered. Robert "Firecracker" Overacker died in 1995 after attempting the descent on a jet ski with a malfunctioning rocket-propelled parachute.

Fifteen intentional plunges over the Canadian Horseshoe Falls have been recorded since 1901. Notably, daredevils avoid the American Falls. Its shallower flow and jagged rock formations below make survival even less likely. Even recklessness has preferences.

Meanwhile, tightrope walkers returned in cycles. Blondin's feats were followed by Maria Spelterini, who crossed the gorge in 1876, once blindfolded and once with baskets strapped to her feet. In 2012, Nik Wallenda crossed near the brink of Horseshoe Falls under special permission from both governments, his passport required upon arrival on the Canadian side. The spectacle remained modern, televised, regulated.

The psychology of these acts is layered.

Standing near the brink, one feels scale. The body registers vibration. The mind registers insignificance. To survive the descent is to invert that equation, to prove that human ingenuity can navigate chaos. Barrels became capsules of defiance, fragile declarations against gravity.

But beneath the legend lay economic calculation. Many attempted the plunge seeking money, sponsorship, or publicity. Few achieved lasting prosperity. Some paid with their lives. The line between performance and tragedy was thin and frequently crossed.

Newspapers serialized the build-up to each attempt. Vendors sold commemorative photographs. Crowds assembled with anticipation sharpened by danger. The water did what it always does. It fell. The rest was human projection.

By the twentieth century, spectacle evolved from improvised daring to curated experience.

Illumination began in the late nineteenth century and expanded with advancing electrical systems. Colored lights transformed the cascade into programmable display. Fireworks punctuated holidays. Tour boats approached the base in choreographed arcs, passengers wrapped in plastic ponchos rehearsing proximity to power without surrendering to it.

Risk, once lethal and spontaneous, became managed.

Yet the legacy of the daredevils remains embedded in Niagara's identity. Museums display barrels like relics. Tour guides recount names with theatrical pause. The narrative reinforces a certain strain of North American audacity, the belief that spectacle invites participation.

Niagara Falls did not invent that impulse. It amplified it.

The city's reputation benefited and complicated itself through these acts. On one hand, daring reinforced global recognition. On the other, it risked reducing a layered community to carnival shorthand.

Beneath the tightrope cables and barrel hoops, deeper transformations were already underway. Engineers were preparing to harness the same force that daredevils treated as adversary. Industry would soon dwarf individual stunts in scale and consequence.

But for a time, the most dramatic confrontations at the brink were singular.

A lone figure against the roar.

The Falls do not remember names. They erase footprints quickly. Yet human memory clings to those who stepped forward rather than back.

Niagara's reputation as a place of risk endures not because the water invites recklessness, but because it magnifies resolve. The gorge is indifferent. The current is constant. It is people who decide to test themselves against it.

Some come to witness. Some come to wager.

The water keeps falling.

Annie Taylor

Mist and Matrimony

Niagara Falls as the Honeymoon Capital

Niagara Falls did not invent the honeymoon.

But it gave it a stage.

The association between Niagara and newlyweds is often traced to a pair of early, high-profile visits. In 1801, Theodosia Burr Alston, daughter of Aaron Burr, traveled to the Falls with her husband shortly after their wedding. Two years later, in 1803, Jérôme Bonaparte, brother of Napoleon, brought his new bride to Niagara. These stories linger because they are tidy: famous names, dramatic landscape, romantic implication.

But historians urge caution.

Elizabeth McKinsey places the true "honeymoon craze" later, in the late 1830s, when scattered references in travel accounts begin explicitly mentioning honeymooners at the Falls. By then, the custom of post-wedding travel was solidifying among America's growing middle and upper classes. Niagara did not create the ritual. It amplified it.

The timing was not accidental.

The tourist industry at Niagara began almost immediately after the War of 1812. In 1822, a Buffalo entrepreneur built the first major hotel at the Falls, the six-story Pavilion on the Canadian side. He promptly fenced his property so that only paying guests could access his privileged view. The sublime acquired a gate.

On the American side, the Eagle Hotel soon followed. Then infrastructure accelerated. The Erie Canal opened in 1825, funneling travelers westward. The Welland Canal followed in 1832, improving navigation around the Falls. Railroads and international bridges in the 1840s and 1850s tightened access further.

By the 1840s, Niagara Falls was receiving roughly 40,000 visitors annually.

A destination had become an itinerary.

Before the Civil War, the Southern aristocracy made seasonal pilgrimages north to escape summer heat and to see and be seen among the American elite. Niagara became a regular stop on what was known as the "Northern Tour," an American analogue to Europe's Grand Tour. Visitors paired the Falls with Quebec City, New York, and Boston, weaving natural spectacle into social calendar.

In that culture of display and refinement, Niagara offered more than scenery. It offered scale. It offered emotion.

By mid-century, honeymoon references appear frequently in travel writing. Newlyweds stood at the brink as mist drifted across silk and wool. Hotels marketed suites and private carriage rides. Photographers staged couples against painted backdrops of the cataract. Romance and commerce learned to cooperate.

The symbolism fit.

The Falls are loud, relentless, and enduring. Marriage promises endurance. The water plunges without hesitation. Couples promised constancy before a force that seemed eternal.

By the late nineteenth century, Niagara Falls was widely described as the "Honeymoon Capital of the World." The phrase stuck because the ritual stuck. Generations of couples made the journey, reinforcing the myth through repetition.

Even as travel diversified in the twentieth century, Niagara retained its romantic imprint. Films, postcards, and popular culture preserved the association. The setting required no explanation. Stand together at the railing. Feel the tremor beneath your feet. Begin something large.

Niagara Falls did not script romance.

It provided thunder for it.

CROSSING THE CURRENT

The Underground Railroad and the Niagara Movement

Niagara Falls, one of the world's most breathtaking natural wonders, holds another legacy beneath its mist. In the nineteenth century, it became a crucial stop on the Underground Railroad, the resistance network that enabled enslaved African Americans to escape bondage and claim freedom. Later, the same border landscape would give its name to a bold civil rights campaign: the Niagara Movement.

The water was loud.

The work was quiet.

The Underground Railroad was not an actual railroad but a broad, evolving resistance to enslavement through escape and flight. Wherever slavery existed, there were efforts to break from it. Early acts of self-emancipation led to maroon communities hidden in remote terrain. Over time, escape routes extended across state lines and international borders. Though enslaved individuals were labeled "fugitives" or "runaways," the term "freedom seeker" better captures their intent.

Many began their journey unaided. Many completed it alone. Yet with each passing decade, especially after the Fugitive Slave Act of 1850, assistance networks expanded. The decision to help a freedom seeker might be spontaneous—a meal offered, a door opened—or deliberate and organized. People of all races, classes, and genders participated in this widespread act of civil disobedience. Freedom seekers traveled toward Canada, Mexico, Spanish Florida, Indian Territory, the West, Caribbean islands, and even Europe. But for thousands, the most decisive threshold lay at the Niagara River.

Niagara Falls mattered because of geography.

Positioned on the border between the United States and Canada, it became a vital crossing point. Once across the river into British Canada, fugitives could no longer be legally returned under American law. The distance was short. The consequence was immense.

Crossings took courage. Some freedom seekers reached the upper river and crossed via the International Suspension Bridge after its completion in 1855, blending into rail traffic. Others moved toward Lewiston or Youngstown and secured covert boat passage across the lower river at night. The current was swift. Patrols were vigilant. Capture meant violence or re-enslavement.

Yet thousands succeeded.

Among the most renowned conductors associated with the Niagara frontier was Harriet Tubman. *(Below)* Tubman, having escaped slavery herself,

Opposite: 1855 -Niagara Falls Suspension Bridge bridge's lower deck entrance. Some enslaved African-Americans used this bridge to Canada in their final steps to freedom.

RATES OF TOLL
AT THIS BRIIGE.

returned repeatedly to guide others north. She once reflected, "I was the conductor of the Underground Railroad for eight years, and I can say what most conductors can't say — I never ran my train off the track and I never lost a passenger." Her routes carried freedom seekers through New York toward Canada, including crossings near Niagara. Her discipline, intelligence, and resolve saved lives.

Another powerful narrative belongs to Josiah Henson, who escaped with his wife and children, crossing into Canada near the Niagara frontier. Henson later became a minister and abolitionist, advocating education and self-determination. His journey testified to endurance shaped by risk.

Niagara Falls itself housed critical safe havens. The Cataract House hotel became one of the most significant Underground Railroad stations in the nation. African American waiters working there quietly organized crossings, guiding fugitives through the hotel and onward to the river. Publicly they served elite tourists. Privately they engineered liberation.

The roar of the Falls concealed movement. The border clarified destiny.

Decades later, the same frontier inspired a new form of resistance. In 1905, W. E. B. Du Bois and fellow activists convened near the Falls, ultimately meeting on the Canadian side after facing discrimination in the United States. They named their organization the Niagara Movement, invoking the Falls' force as metaphor for uncompromising civil rights advocacy.

Where the Underground Railroad embodied escape, the Niagara Movement embodied insistence.

Niagara has long been a threshold—between bondage and freedom, exclusion and demand.

The water falls.

People cross.

Justice gathers force.

The spectacle was impressive. The math was irresistible.

1905- The Niagara Movement. some of the attendees at the first Niagara Conference.

When Water Became Wire

By the late nineteenth century, Niagara Falls had been sketched, painted, fenced, preserved, and risked. But one question pressed harder than the mist against a visitor's coat: What if this falling water could do more than inspire?

For decades, inventors had tried to tap the Falls' energy. Early mills diverted small portions of the river into canals that powered mechanical shafts. The output was local, limited by friction and distance. Energy traveled only as far as belts and gears could carry it.

The breakthrough required abstraction.

Enter Nikola Tesla, *(left)* whose work on alternating current proposed something radical for its time: electricity that could travel long distances without catastrophic loss. Direct current systems, championed by Thomas Edison, were constrained by proximity. Alternating current promised reach.

Entrepreneur George Westinghouse recognized the stakes. He secured patents, invested capital, and aligned himself with Tesla's system. The newly formed Niagara Falls Power Company sought proposals to harness the cataract at scale. The challenge was enormous. Divert enough water to generate substantial electricity, yet preserve the scenic integrity that tourism depended upon.

Engineering became negotiation.

The Edward Dean Adams Power Plant, completed in 1895, represented a technological pivot point. Massive underground tunnels channeled water from the upper river to turbines housed below ground. After spinning generators, the water was discharged downstream through a tailrace tunnel that exited into the gorge.

It was industrial invisibility by design.

Visitors at the brink still saw water flowing. Beneath their feet, a portion of that flow had been rerouted into copper and steel. In 1896, electricity generated at Niagara traveled 20 miles to Buffalo, lighting streetcars and factories. The experiment worked. The War of Currents tilted decisively toward alternating current.

Niagara Falls became proof.

Industry responded quickly. Electrochemical processes that had once been geographically constrained now clustered near cheap power. Aluminum refining required immense electrical input. So did the production of chlorine and other chemical compounds. Factories rose along Buffalo Avenue and the river corridor. Brick by brick, the skyline thickened.

The Falls had always roared. Now they hummed.

Immigrant labor fueled expansion. Workers arrived from Italy, Poland, Germany, Ireland, Eastern Europe. Neighborhoods formed around shift schedules and factory whistles. Churches and corner stores followed payrolls. The city's identity shifted from scenic outpost to industrial engine.

Hydropower offered competitive advantage. Electricity from Niagara cost less than coal-fired alternatives. Manufacturers understood arithmetic. Concentration intensified.

By the early twentieth century, Niagara Falls ranked among the most industrialized cities per capita in the nation. The very force that once inspired painters now drove arc furnaces. Smoke plumes joined mist in the skyline.

World War I accelerated production. Chemical plants supplied materials essential to military manufacturing. World War II repeated the surge. Expansion felt permanent. Infrastructure scaled accordingly.

Mid-century ambition culminated in the construction of the Robert Moses Niagara Power Plant under the authority of the New York Power Authority. Completed in 1961 after a catastrophic rockslide destroyed its predecessor, the plant diverted even greater volumes of water through massive conduits carved into bedrock.

The spectacle remained for tourists. The machinery grew colossal beyond view.

Hydropower made Niagara Falls synonymous with modern infrastructure. The city exported electricity far beyond its borders. The river became both scenic icon and energy backbone for the region.

But abundance carries shadow.

Cheap electricity encouraged energy-intensive industries whose byproducts were less visible than turbines. Waste disposal practices lagged behind production capacity. Regulation remained light. The emphasis was output, not aftermath.

For decades, the arrangement appeared efficient. Power flowed. Jobs remained steady. The city prospered.

Yet dependence on a narrow industrial base made Niagara Falls vulnerable. When global competition intensified and manufacturing began to contract in the 1970s, closures cascaded. Plants shuttered. Payrolls thinned. The turbines continued to spin, but fewer local workers benefited directly from their output.

Hydropower outlasted industry.

In the twenty-first century, the narrative has shifted again. Renewable energy advocates point to Niagara's hydroelectric capacity as early proof that large-scale clean energy is feasible. The same river that powered chlorine plants now contributes to lower-carbon grids.

Still, the history is layered.

When water became wire, Niagara Falls entered the modern age with voltage in its veins. The achievement was undeniable. It electrified cities, reshaped industry, and anchored regional growth. It also concentrated environmental risk and economic dependency.

The river does not choose its uses.

It falls. It flows. It turns turbines when directed. It erodes stone when ignored.

Niagara Falls proved that nature's force could be translated into infrastructure. The harder lesson, still unfolding, is how to balance innovation with foresight.

The roar remains constant.

The wiring around it keeps evolving.

Into the Spray

The History of the Maid of the Mist

You can look at Niagara Falls from above.

Or you can sail into it.

Since 1846, the Maid of the Mist has offered the second option.

The Maid of the Mist is a sightseeing boat tour operating from Niagara Falls, New York. The voyage begins and ends on the American side, briefly crossing into Canadian waters as it approaches the base of the Horseshoe Falls. Today it is a ritual. Ponchos snap in the wind. Cameras fog. Passengers lean into the spray.

But the story began not as spectacle, but as transportation.

Ferry Before Fame

The original Maid of the Mist was built at a landing on the American side and christened in 1846. Its first voyage took place on September 18 of that year. It was not designed as a tourist attraction. It was a border-crossing ferry.

The vessel was a 72-foot wooden side-wheeler, 18 feet wide, powered by steam generated from wood and coal. It could carry up to 100 passengers. The intention was practical: to serve as a link in a broader ferry connection between New York City and Toronto.

For two years, it worked.

Then in 1848, a suspension bridge opened across the Niagara River, diverting cross-border traffic. The ferry's economic purpose dissolved almost overnight. Faced with obsolescence, the owners made a pivot that would define Niagara tourism for generations.

If the boat could no longer carry people across the river, it could carry them toward the Falls.

The ferry became an attraction.

A Name from Legend

The name "Maid of the Mist" likely draws from the Iroquois legend of Lelawala, a young woman said to have been carried over the Falls and into the realm of the Thunder God. Whether myth or marketing, the name fused natural force with narrative.

It suggested surrender to power. It promised proximity to something ancient.

That promise sold.

Reinvention and Expansion

In 1884, Captain R. F. Carter and Frank LaBlond formed the present-day Maid of the Mist Corporation. They invested in a new vessel, launched in 1885 and built by Alfred H. White of Port Robinson, Ontario. The service professionalized. Boats were purpose-built for sightseeing rather than transport.

Through the late nineteenth and early twentieth centuries, steam-powered wooden-hulled boats carried visitors into the basin below the Falls. They became icons of the Niagara experience.

In 1955, an early-season fire destroyed the last of the wooden steamers. That same year, diesel-powered vessels replaced them, marking a technological shift but preserving the core experience.

The boats grew larger. The crowds grew denser. The ritual endured.

Modern Stewardship

Since 1971, the Maid of the Mist has been owned by the Glynn family. Under the leadership of James V. Glynn, the operation expanded significantly, including the construction of multiple new vessels.

Maid of the Mist II, 1896–1906

The embarkation point on the American side is reached by four elevators descending through an observation tower to the dock below. It feels ceremonial: a descent into anticipation.

The boats depart, edge past the American Falls, and then turn toward the Horseshoe Falls, where water crashes with a force measured in millions of gallons per minute. The engines strain forward. Spray engulfs the deck. The roar becomes physical.

And then, just as quickly, the vessel pivots and returns.

Notable Passengers

The Maid of the Mist has hosted heads of state and royalty. Mikhail Gorbachev rode in 1983. In 1991, Prince Charles and Princess Diana, accompanied by Princes William and Harry, boarded the boat. In 1996, former U.S. President Jimmy Carter sailed into the mist.

They all wore ponchos.

Power reduces everyone to equal footing at the base of the Falls.

Enduring Icon

There have been sightseeing boats at Niagara since 1846. Generations have stood on their decks. Technology has evolved from wood-fired steam to diesel and beyond. Ownership has changed hands. Borders have shifted.

The experience remains elemental.

The Maid of the Mist survives because it answers a simple desire: not just to see Niagara Falls, but to feel it.

You can admire the water from above.

Or you can ride into the thunder.

14 22

Steel Beside the Torrent

The Great Gorge Route

There was a time when you could ride a trolley at water level through the Niagara Gorge, so close to the river that spray misted your sleeves and the roar pressed against your ribs.

It was called the Great Gorge Route.

Officially, the Niagara Gorge Railroad formed the American portion of this system, an interurban railway that ran at the bottom of the gorge from Niagara Falls, New York to Lewiston, New York. It operated from 1895 until 1935, hugging the base of cliffs that were still actively crumbling. The idea bordered on audacious.

Building the Impossible

The original company, the Niagara Falls and Whirlpool Company, formed in 1886 with plans to build a narrow-gauge line from Prospect Point to just north of the Whirlpool. It went bankrupt before construction began.

Two Buffalo businessmen, Captain George M. Brinker and George A. Ricker, reorganized the effort as the Niagara Falls and Lewiston Railroad. Construction began on April 11, 1895. The line opened just seventy-five days later, on August 25.

Seventy-five days.

Workers blasted and carved a ten-foot-wide rail bed into the gorge wall. In the first half mile alone, 100,000 cubic yards of rock were dumped into the Niagara River. The full route extended seven miles. Only 700 feet were level ground. The rest curved and climbed at grades as steep as nine percent.

It was one of the most difficult rail projects ever attempted in North America.

And it became an instant sensation.

Stations Along the Roar

The railroad ran from Niagara Falls to Lewiston at water level, stopping at stations with names that read like a travelogue of the gorge: International Railway Terminal, Great Gorge Route Ticket Office, New York Central Depot, Schoellkopf Station, Rapids View, Whirlpool Rapids, Whirlpool Point, Ongiara Park, Giant Rock, Devil's Hole, Lewiston–Queenston Bridge, and Lewiston Dock.

In Niagara Falls, passengers connected to the International Railway Company, New York Central, Erie Railroad, Canadian National, and Lehigh Valley. At Lewiston Dock, they transferred to New York Central lines, the Lewiston & Youngstown Frontier, and Canada Steamship Lines steamers bound for Toronto.

Lewiston, already a historic port of entry since 1811, surged again as tourists arrived by boat from Toronto and Montreal, transferring directly to the gorge trolley for the ride south to the Falls.

The railroad did more than move passengers. It rearranged the region's transportation economy.

An International Loop

By 1899, financial strain forced Brinker to sell the line. Under new ownership, it became the Niagara Gorge Railroad. In 1902, it merged with the Canadian Niagara Falls Park & River Railway, forming an international belt known as the "Niagara Gorge Belt Line" or simply the Great Gorge Route.

Passengers could board at the Canadian end of the Upper Steel Arch Bridge, ride south past the American Falls to Table Rock at Horseshoe Falls, loop north through Queen Victoria Park, cross into Lewiston via the Queenston–Lewiston Suspension Bridge, and then descend again to the river's edge.

It was a six-mile electric loop. Open-sided summer trolleys carried riders within feet of the Whirlpool Rapids. Conductors walked along running boards collecting fares as the cars moved. The experience

rivaled the Falls themselves.

After five years, cars ran every fifteen minutes from 7 a.m. to midnight, ten months a year. The line closed each spring during thaw season, when rockslides were most likely.

In forty years, the Great Gorge Route carried roughly thirteen million passengers.

Triumph and Tragedy

Engineering bravado met geological reality.

Rockfalls were frequent. In 1899, a thousand-ton slide near the American Falls swept away sections of track. Engineers planted quackroot grass to stabilize slopes. Repairs became routine and expensive.

Remarkably, for decades no passenger or employee was struck by falling rock.

But accidents came from other causes.

In 1907, an avalanche of ice killed a conductor and eight passengers. In 1915, a trolley overloaded with 157 Sunday school picnickers from Toronto derailed on a wet escarpment curve near Queenston Heights. Thirteen died. In 1917, a car plunged into the river near the Whirlpool Rapids after heavy rains undermined the rail bed. Twelve more died.

The gorge was beautiful. It was not forgiving.

Still, dignitaries rode the line. On September 6, 1901, President William McKinley traveled from Lewiston to Niagara Falls via the Great Gorge Route. Hours later, he was assassinated in Buffalo.

The End of the Line

The automobile changed everything.

By the 1920s and early 1930s, passenger numbers dwindled. The Canadian portion closed in 1932. The American side struggled on.

At 2 a.m. on September 17, 1935, more than five thousand tons of rock crashed down just north of the Whirlpool Bridge, destroying over 200 feet of track and rail bed. It was the largest rockfall in the railroad's history.

This time, repairs did not follow.

The Great Gorge Route shut down immediately and permanently.

What Remains

Today, the Great Gorge Railway Trail follows portions of the former route. Brick supports and fragments of rail bed linger at the base of the gorge, half reclaimed by moss and vine.

The Industrial Revolution made the Great Gorge Route possible. The automobile made it obsolete. And the gorge itself ensured its vulnerability.

For forty years, steel clung to cliff face, and passengers rode at the edge of the torrent. The trolley bells have been silent since 1935.

The river keeps running.

The gorge keeps shedding stone.

Nature reclaims what steel once claimed.

If you walk the trail today, you can still imagine it: open-sided cars, wind in your face, the conductor balancing along a narrow board, and the Whirlpool Rapids raging just below.

An engineering marvel.

A gamble against gravity.

A railroad that dared to run beside thunder.

Cave of the Winds

Walking Into the Power of Niagara

Few experiences at Niagara Falls bring visitors as close to the raw force of nature as the famous Cave of the Winds. Today, tourists don ponchos and climb wooden walkways beside the roaring Bridal Veil Falls, but the attraction began nearly two centuries ago as a mysterious natural cavern hidden behind the waterfall itself.

The story begins in 1834, when writer and early travel guide author Joseph W. Ingraham discovered a remarkable cave tucked behind the thin veil of water cascading from Bridal Veil Falls. The cavern sat directly beneath the towering cliffs of Goat Island, carved by centuries of rushing water and erosion. Ingraham named the discovery Aeolus' Cave, after the Greek god of the winds, because of the extraordinary blasts of air produced by the waterfall. Inside the cavern, powerful drafts created by the falling water could reach 68 miles per hour, whipping through the dark chamber like a constant storm.

Not long after its discovery, two explorers—Barry Hill White and George Sims—became the first known visitors to venture inside the cave. What they found was both thrilling and unsettling. The cavern echoed with thunderous noise, swirling mist, and powerful gusts of wind. Yet the dramatic experience quickly captured the imagination of early Niagara Falls tourists.

Access to the gorge had already begun to improve. In 1829, years before the cave's discovery, Porter Biddle had constructed a steep

488—Cave of the Winds.

wooden stairway down the cliffs of Goat Island known as the Biddle Staircase. This stairway allowed adventurous visitors to descend toward the river below. Once the cave became known, entrepreneurs soon realized its potential as a tourist attraction.

By 1841, guided tours into the cave were officially offered to the public. Visitors would descend the Biddle Staircase and carefully navigate the slippery rocks before entering the cavern behind the waterfall. The experience was unforgettable. Standing inside the cave, tourists could look outward through the curtain of water while feeling the wind and spray created by the powerful falls.

For decades, the Cave of the Winds became one of Niagara's most popular attractions. Victorian-era visitors described the sensation as standing inside a living storm. However, the cave's dramatic beauty came with serious dangers. The cliffs of the Niagara Gorge are composed of layers of limestone resting on softer shale, making them prone to sudden rockfalls.

Those dangers became tragically clear in 1920, when a rockfall inside the cave killed three visitors. After the accident, authorities closed the original cave permanently due to safety concerns.

Despite the closure, the attraction itself did not disappear. In 1924, a new concept was introduced. Instead of entering the cave behind the falls, visitors would experience the power of Bridal Veil Falls from a network of wooden decks and walkways built along the cliff face in front of the waterfall. This new design allowed people to approach the cascading water safely while still experiencing its intensity.

The following year, in 1925, a major improvement replaced the aging Biddle Staircase. Engineers carved an elevator shaft through 170 feet of solid rock, allowing visitors to descend quickly from Goat Island to the base of the gorge.

Nature delivered the final chapter for the original cave in 1954, when a massive rockfall nearly destroyed what remained of the cavern. The following year, engineers deliberately dynamited the unstable overhang to prevent further danger. With that action, the physical cave itself disappeared forever.

Yet the spirit of the attraction lived on. Today's Cave of the Winds remains one of Niagara Falls State Park's most thrilling experiences. Visitors descend by elevator before walking along a series of wooden platforms built at the base of Bridal Veil Falls. The most famous section, known as the Hurricane Deck, places visitors within about 20 feet of the roaring waterfall, where powerful gusts of wind and crashing water recreate the storm-like conditions that inspired the cave's original name.

Each year, the wooden walkways are dismantled in autumn to prevent damage from winter ice and rebuilt by hand every spring. The modern experience begins at the World Changed Here Pavilion, where exhibits introduce visitors to the natural and technological history of Niagara Falls.

Although the cave itself no longer exists, the experience it inspired continues to bring visitors face to face with the breathtaking power of Niagara. The Cave of the Winds remains a place where people can quite literally walk into the thunder of the falls.

Opposite: 19th century photograph of the entrance to Cave of the Winds

Whiskey on Ice

Temperance and Prohibition in Niagara Falls

Long before the era of national Prohibition, travelers moving through nineteenth-century America often faced a simple but uncomfortable reality: most lodging houses were closely tied to alcohol. Public houses and taverns frequently doubled as inns, providing beds upstairs and lively barrooms below. These establishments were social centers as much as they were places to sleep. Laughter, arguments, card games, and the steady clink of glassware were common features of the traveler's night.

For many visitors, this atmosphere was simply part of the road. But for others, particularly families, ministers, and those aligned with the growing Temperance Movement, it could make travel unpredictable. One might arrive weary from a long journey only to find the night's accommodations attached to a crowded barroom thick with smoke and drink.

Temperance House - Falls and Second Streets -1919

The situation was hardly unique to Niagara Falls. Across the United States and Europe, the close relationship between lodging and alcohol had long been standard practice. Taverns provided meals, stabling, and beds, but the bar was almost always the heart of the establishment. Hotels that emerged in growing cities often adopted a similar arrangement. Even grand hotels featured large public barrooms where guests and locals mingled.

For travelers hoping to avoid encounters with public drinking, reformers and entrepreneurs began offering an alternative: the Temperance hotel.

Originating in Great Britain as early as 1833, Temperance hotels were designed to provide respectable lodging without alcohol. These establishments were promoted as safe, wholesome environments where guests could eat, rest, and socialize without the influence of drink. Dining rooms replaced bar counters as gathering spaces. Tea, coffee, and conversation substituted for whiskey and ale.

The concept traveled quickly across the Atlantic alongside the broader Temperance Movement. By the mid-nineteenth century, temperance societies were active in many American cities, including Buffalo and Niagara Falls. Hotels aligned with the movement appealed to ministers, reformers, families, and travelers who preferred a quieter atmosphere.

In a tourist destination like Niagara Falls, such accommodations had particular appeal. Visitors came from around the world to witness the thunder of the cataract and the spectacle of the gorge. Not all of them wanted their evenings spent navigating crowded drinking rooms. Temperance hotels offered a different kind of hospitality, one rooted in moral reform and social respectability.

Yet the broader culture of drinking never disappeared. The Falls region, like much of North America, remained a place where taverns, saloons, and hotel bars flourished alongside reform movements.

That tension between temperance and indulgence would reach its most dramatic chapter in the early twentieth century.

When the Nation Went Dry

When the United States went dry in 1920, Niagara Falls did not.

It adapted.

The Eighteenth Amendment outlawed the manufacture and sale of alcohol. The Volstead Act enforced it. Across much of the country, bootlegging required hidden warehouses, elaborate distribution networks, and long-distance transport.

In Niagara Falls, it required a river.

And sometimes, in winter, it required ice.

A Border Made for Opportunity

The Niagara River has always been more than scenery. It is a boundary, a channel of commerce, and a line on a map that becomes negotiable when viewed from the right angle.

Canada did not adopt national Prohibition in the same way the United States did. Liquor production continued, and export remained legal. Meanwhile, demand south of the border surged almost overnight.

Geography handled the rest.

Small boats slipped across the river under cover of darkness. Automobiles crossed the Honeymoon Bridge and the Queenston–Lewiston Bridge carrying concealed cargo. Rail shipments blurred paperwork and destination labels.

Model T truck breaks through the river ice with an overload of Canadian liquor

The constant thunder of the Falls masked many sounds.

Niagara Falls quickly became a convenient funnel for liquor moving from Ontario into New York and beyond. What began as opportunism gradually evolved into organized networks. Rum-running was not always glamorous. More often it was quiet and methodical. A trunk full of bottles. A discreet bribe. A crate transferred silently along a dock.

Ice Bridges: Winter's Shortcut

Winter brought a new dimension to the trade.

During especially cold seasons, the lower Niagara River could freeze solid enough to form what locals called an "ice bridge." Massive slabs of ice locked together below the Falls, stretching from the American shore to the Canadian side.

Tourists once ventured onto these frozen expanses for novelty photographs.

Bootleggers saw something else entirely.

When the ice thickened, smugglers could haul cases of liquor across the frozen river by sled or on foot. There were no engines, no wakes, no mechanical noise. Just the sound of boots crunching across blue-white slabs under moonlight.

The ice bridge transformed the international border into a temporary sidewalk.

It was dangerous work. The ice could shift or fracture without warning. But risk and reward often travel together. In a border town, adaptation is survival. When the river flowed, boats moved. When it froze, men walked.

Federal agents understood this well. Patrols increased during freeze seasons. Still, the gorge is wide, and the night is generous.

Speakeasies Beneath the Mist

Within the city of Niagara Falls, enforcement often fluctuated.

Speakeasies appeared behind false storefronts and inside hotel basements. Passwords were whispered at doors. Bottles were hidden in walls and beneath floorboards. Patrons sipped Canadian whiskey within earshot of American law. The irony was thick as the mist rising from the cataract.

Hotels that once served alcohol openly adapted to coded service. Bartenders learned discretion. Police raids occurred, though not always consistently. Tourism mattered. Public image mattered. A border town learns to balance principle with practicality.

For many residents, rum-running was not a profession but a supplement. Industrial wages fluctuated, and winters could be slow. Moving a few cases across the river might mean groceries paid for and heat in the house.

The water powered turbines.

The water also powered sideline economies.

Repeal and Memory

When Prohibition ended in 1933, legal alcohol returned with relief and celebration. Speakeasies rebranded as bars. Smuggling networks dissolved or redirected their efforts.

But the habits of adaptation remained.

Niagara Falls had once again proven itself a place where national policy met local geography and bent slightly. The river carried more than tourists and electricity. For thirteen years it carried whiskey, risk, and quiet improvisation.

The ice bridges eventually disappeared as river control projects and changing winter conditions altered the flow of ice below the Falls. Yet for a brief and remarkable period, the border quite literally froze beneath people's feet.

Water hardened.

Boots crossed.

Bottles changed hands.

HOTEL

When the River Took the Bridge

The Honeymoon Bridge Collapse

Niagara Falls is accustomed to spectacle.

But on the morning of January 27, 1938, the spectacle turned structural.

The Honeymoon Bridge, officially known as the Upper Steel Arch Bridge, had spanned the Niagara River just downstream from the American Falls since 1898. Graceful and utilitarian, its steel arch stretched across the gorge near where the Rainbow Bridge stands today. It carried trolley cars, automobiles, and pedestrians between the United States and Canada. It was a working bridge, not a stunt. It existed for movement, not applause.

And then winter arrived with authority.

The winter of 1937 to 1938 was severe. Ice built thick along the upper river, pressing toward the brink. When shifting winds and water levels destabilized the ice jam, enormous slabs surged over the Falls and into the gorge below. The Honeymoon Bridge found itself under assault not from traffic, but from geology.

Ice is quiet when it forms. It is not quiet when it moves.

By late January, massive fields of ice had lodged against the bridge's lower structure. Pressure mounted. Steel groaned. Observers gathered along the banks, drawn by rumor and tension. They had seen ice before. They had not seen it accumulate like this.

On January 27, under the weight of thousands of tons of frozen river, the arch began to give way. The south anchor shifted first. Then the entire steel span buckled. In dramatic sequence, the bridge collapsed into the gorge.

No lives were lost. Traffic had been halted as the danger became evident. But the sight stunned the region. A structure that had endured forty years of weather and weight surrendered in hours to ice.

The image traveled widely: twisted steel submerged in a white churn of ice floes. The Falls thundered on, unchanged. The bridge was gone.

The collapse was not merely an engineering failure. It was a reminder of hierarchy. Human design can span a gorge. It cannot negotiate indefinitely with the river.

For Niagara Falls, the bridge had been more than infrastructure. It was a symbol of connection. It carried commerce and daily routine. It linked two nations in ordinary ways: work commutes, shopping trips, afternoon strolls.

Its sudden disappearance felt like interruption.

Yet Niagara Falls does not linger long in interruption.

Within two years, a replacement rose: the Rainbow Bridge, opened in 1941. Positioned slightly upstream from the Honeymoon Bridge's original site, the new structure reflected lessons learned. Its steel arch sat higher above the river, accounting for ice flow and clearance. It was engineered with winter in mind.

Where the Honeymoon Bridge had fallen, the Rainbow Bridge stood prepared.

The collapse of 1938 remains one of Niagara Falls' quieter disasters. It did not involve daring or scandal. It involved physics. Ice, weight, leverage.

But it fits the city's larger story.

Niagara Falls has built boldly beside power for two centuries. Hydroelectric plants, hotels, armories, casinos, malls, and monuments all exist in negotiation with the river. The Honeymoon Bridge collapse reminds us that negotiation has limits.

The water shapes the gorge.

The ice tests the steel.

The city rebuilds.

Architecture here is always provisional.

Between Thunder & Transaction

Commerce in the Shadow of the Falls

Every city has two economies.

The one visitors see.

And the one that pays the mortgage.

In Niagara Falls, those economies have always overlapped, collided, and occasionally misunderstood each other. One is powered by spectacle. The other by necessity. One rises and falls with tourism cycles. The other depends on grocery lists, paydays, and winter.

To understand retail and business in Niagara Falls is to understand a city that has always stood between thunder and transaction.

Mills, Main Street, and the Making of a Commercial Spine

Before souvenir shops and neon signs, commerce in Niagara Falls followed waterpower.

In the nineteenth century, the roar of the river attracted more than tourists. It drew mill operators and industrialists who understood what the Niagara River offered: abundant hydroelectric energy, continuous motion, and proximity to shipping routes connecting the Great Lakes to the interior of the continent. Factories grew along the river and canal systems, and with them came workers who needed places to buy boots, flour, tools, fabric, and household necessities.

Retail followed labor.

Small mercantile shops clustered near the industrial corridors, serving workers who clocked out coated in grain dust, grease, or chemical residue. As the population expanded in the late nineteenth and early twentieth centuries, commerce gradually organized itself along several primary streets.

Main Street became the backbone of everyday commerce. Pine Avenue developed as a lively neighborhood business district, especially among Italian immigrant families who opened bakeries, butcher shops, cafés, and specialty groceries. Falls Street, leading directly toward the cataract itself, developed a dual personality, serving both residents and the growing number of visitors arriving to witness the natural wonder.

By the early twentieth century these streets formed the city's commercial spine.

Storefronts multiplied. Department stores rose along busy blocks. Cinemas, banks, pharmacies, restaurants, and clothing shops filled the spaces between. Saturdays meant sidewalks crowded with families carrying parcels wrapped in brown paper and tied with string. During the holidays, department store windows became miniature stages filled with electric lights, toy trains, and snowy winter scenes.

This was not tourist retail.

It was civic retail.

It was a middle-class ecosystem supported by factory payrolls and anchored by habit. Workers from nearby chemical plants, hydroelectric facilities, and manufacturing shops shopped downtown not because it was charming but because it was convenient and essential.

The Falls roared in the distance.

Downtown hummed with commerce.

The Golden Age of Downtown Retail

From the 1930s through the 1960s, Niagara Falls, New York had a lively downtown retail district centered primarily along Pine Avenue, Falls Street, and Main Street. The area functioned as the region's primary shopping corridor before suburban malls arrived in the late 1960s. The retailers ranged from large

O'Keefe
ALE
BEER
SEARS
TWO-WAY
TRAFFIC
AHEAD

BERGS
SILBERBERG
Florsheim
SHOE
Silberbergs
FOUR
Silberbergs

department stores to locally owned specialty shops that served both residents and the constant flow of tourists visiting the falls.

Several well-known national and regional retailers anchored the district and gave Niagara Falls the feel of a full-service American shopping center.

Among the most prominent was Hens & Kelly, a regional department store chain with deep Western New York roots. Its Pine Avenue store became a local landmark, offering clothing, housewares, furniture, and seasonal merchandise displayed across multiple floors.

Another major presence was AM&A's (Adam, Meldrum & Anderson), the Buffalo-based department store that expanded to Niagara Falls during the mid-twentieth century. AM&A's offered fashion, cosmetics, furniture, and household goods, bringing a metropolitan department store experience to the city.

J.C. Penney served families seeking dependable and affordable clothing, while Montgomery Ward and Sears supplied appliances, tools, and catalog merchandise reflecting the modern American household.

Five-and-dime stores such as F.W. Woolworth and S.S. Kresge filled an essential niche. Their counters offered inexpensive goods ranging from toys and sewing supplies to candy and kitchen utensils. Their lunch counters became popular gathering spots where teenagers met after school and workers paused for coffee and sandwiches.

Other retailers, including W.T. Grant, shoe stores like Kinney Shoes, jewelry shops, pharmacies, and family-owned boutiques filled the surrounding blocks.

Pine Avenue in particular developed a strong neighborhood identity. Italian bakeries, delicatessens, and specialty grocers served the surrounding community, giving the street an aroma of fresh bread and espresso that lingered long after storefront doors closed for the evening.

Downtown Niagara Falls in these decades was not simply a shopping district. It was a civic stage where daily life unfolded in public.

Selling the Sublime

Parallel to that local economy was a more theatrical one.

By the mid-nineteenth century, Niagara Falls had become one of the most recognizable tourist destinations in the world. Railroads delivered visitors from major cities. Steamships carried travelers across the Great Lakes. Guidebooks listed recommended hotels and scenic viewpoints.

Where visitors gather, commerce multiplies.

Souvenir shops appeared near the park boundary and along Falls Street. Visitors purchased postcards, carved keepsakes, and photographs of the illuminated falls. Miniature barrels referencing famous daredevils became popular novelties. Confectioners packaged fudge in decorative boxes stamped with images of the cataract.

Retail near the Falls trafficked in awe.

Niagara Falls learned to monetize wonder without completely overwhelming it.

Industrial Prosperity and Retail Confidence

During the mid-twentieth century, Niagara Falls' industrial base reached its peak.

Chemical and electrochemical plants such as Hooker Chemical, Union Carbide, and others employed thousands. Hydroelectric power fueled production, and steady wages supported a large middle class.

Retail thrived because paychecks were reliable.

Main Street department stores expanded. Appliance dealers sold refrigerators and

Opposite: Silberberg's Department Store, Main and Ontario Ave after a fire at W.T. Grant store (left). 1936

1965– S.S Kresge Co located on Queen Street

televisions to families moving into new suburban homes. Restaurants filled during shift changes. Movie theaters drew crowds beneath glowing marquees.

Downtown reflected confidence.

The Shift After the 1960s

By the late 1960s and early 1970s, the commercial landscape began to change.

Retail gradually moved away from downtown due to several forces:

- Urban renewal projects that disrupted the traditional street grid
- Construction of suburban shopping plazas designed for automobiles
- The opening of enclosed regional malls such as Summit Park Mall (1972)

As consumers increasingly drove to suburban shopping centers, foot traffic downtown declined. Historic retailers closed or relocated. Department stores that had anchored entire blocks gradually disappeared.

Retail rarely collapses dramatically. It erodes gradually.

A bakery closes.

A clothing shop shortens its hours.

A theater goes dark.

Eventually a district grows quiet.

The Rainbow Centre Experiment

In 1978, the Rainbow Centre Mall opened downtown with the goal of reversing that decline. Designed as a modern enclosed shopping center, it attempted to bring the suburban mall model back into the city core.

For a time it succeeded. Families shopped beneath climate-controlled ceilings, teenagers gathered in food courts, and the mall generated new foot traffic downtown.

But retail trends continued to shift. Larger regional malls competed for customers, cross-border shopping patterns fluctuated, and anchor tenants departed.

By the early 2000s the mall struggled with rising

vacancy. Demolition eventually followed, leaving behind a reminder of both ambition and the difficulty of reshaping retail patterns once they have shifted.

Outlet Retail and the Border Economy

While downtown retail declined, another model found success on the outskirts of the city.

The Niagara Factory Outlet Mall, opened in 1982 and later expanded as the Fashion Outlets of Niagara Falls, capitalized on cross-border shopping and highway access. Canadian visitors frequently crossed the border seeking lower prices and favorable exchange rates.

Unlike traditional downtown retail, the outlet mall functioned as a regional destination. Shoppers arrived by car or tour bus rather than on foot.

The mall proved remarkably resilient, adapting tenant mixes and expanding retail offerings while downtown continued searching for its new identity.

New Anchors in the Twenty-First Century

A major turning point came in 2002 with the opening of the Seneca Niagara Resort & Casino. The casino brought new hospitality jobs, year-round visitors, and renewed investment near the tourism district.

Hotels, restaurants, and entertainment venues followed. Retail around the casino focused less on department stores and more on dining, convenience services, and visitor-oriented businesses.

The commercial landscape evolved again.

Retail Today: Patchwork and Persistence

Retail in Niagara Falls today reflects many layers of history.

Outlet shopping centers attract regional visitors and Canadian shoppers. Downtown continues periodic redevelopment efforts aimed at reconnecting retail with tourism. Restaurants and cafés cluster near the park boundary and casino district.

The City Market of Niagara Falls– 18 St. and Pine Ave. 1914

Meanwhile neighborhood businesses continue their quieter role.

Barber shops, auto repair garages, corner groceries, and family-owned restaurants serve residents regardless of tourism cycles. Entrepreneurs experiment with coffee shops, galleries, and specialty stores hoping to convert proximity to millions of annual visitors into steady commerce.

Winter still matters.

Seasonality shapes staffing and inventory.

E-commerce adds another layer of competition.

Retailers here compete not only with nearby cities but with global online marketplaces.

A City of Commercial Experiments

Niagara Falls has always been a place where commerce stands in the shadow of spectacle. The water guarantees attention. It does not guarantee a sale.

For more than a century, merchants have tested ideas along streets that lead toward the roar. Some businesses flourish. Others fade quietly between tourist seasons. The cycle repeats, generation after generation, as each new wave of entrepreneurs tries to turn passing wonder into a lasting livelihood.

Through it all, the Falls remain unconcerned with retail trends or economic forecasts. The water keeps moving. It plunges over the edge with the same indifference it had when the first souvenir stands appeared and when the first grand hotels lit their windows at night.

The city around that water, however, refuses to stand still.the key in the morning light, flips the sign to OPEN, and gives the idea another day.

Falls Street at Second Ave

The Industrial City Beside the Falls

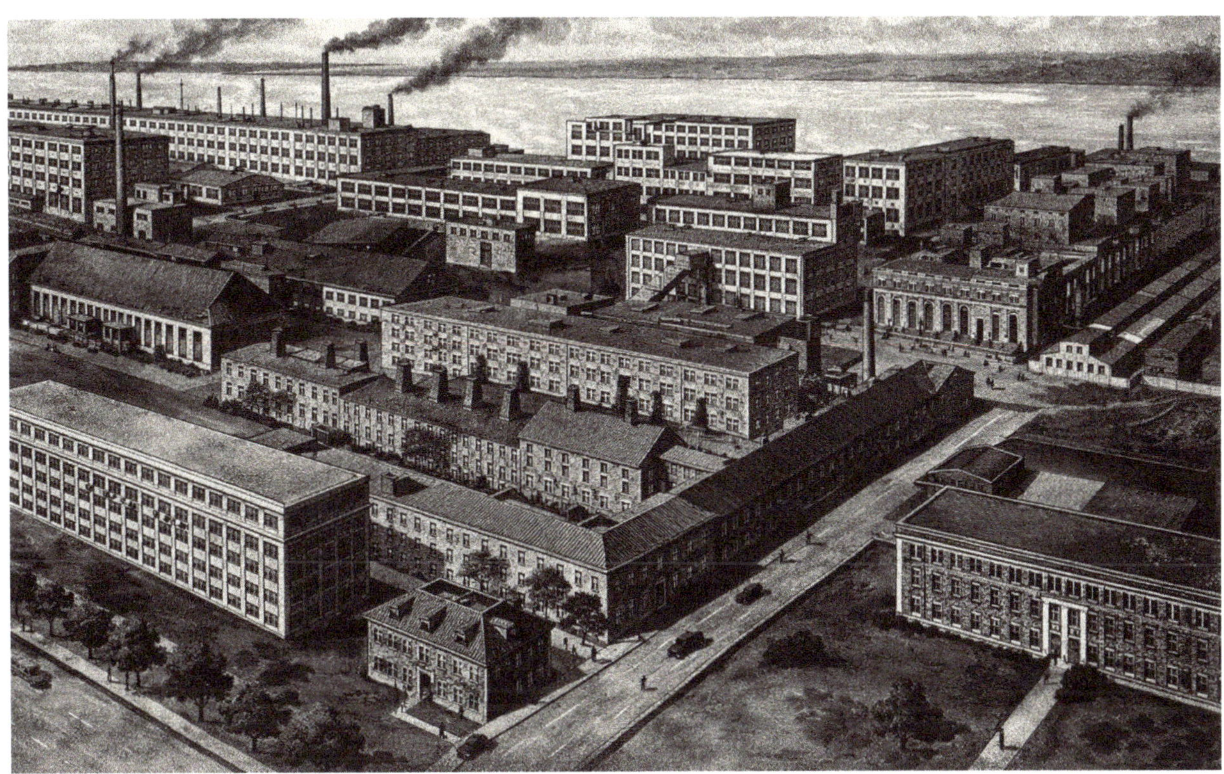

The Carborundum Company site on Buffalo Avenue

Long before Niagara Falls became known primarily as a tourist destination, it was one of the most important industrial centers in North America. The same natural force that drew visitors from around the world—the immense power of the Niagara River—also attracted engineers, investors, and manufacturers who saw the falls as an unparalleled source of energy.

In the nineteenth century, the industrial potential of Niagara Falls began to take shape. Early entrepreneurs recognized that the tremendous volume of water flowing from Lake Erie to Lake Ontario could be harnessed to power mills and factories. Initial efforts were modest. Small canals and hydraulic systems built in the 1850s and 1860s diverted water from the river to turn mechanical turbines. These early systems powered sawmills, flour mills, and a handful of small factories, but they also revealed the immense industrial possibilities of Niagara's waterpower.

The true transformation began in the late nineteenth century with the construction of large-scale hydroelectric systems. The Niagara Falls Hydraulic Power and Manufacturing Company built a canal that diverted water from the Niagara River through turbines before returning it to the gorge. Completed in the 1890s, the project provided enormous amounts of electricity to nearby factories.

In 1895, the Edward Dean Adams Power Station began generating electricity using alternating current technology developed by Nikola Tesla and commercialized by George Westinghouse. The plant successfully transmitted electricity twenty miles to Buffalo, proving that hydroelectric power could supply entire cities and industries. Niagara Falls suddenly possessed one of the cheapest and most reliable energy sources in the world.

Industries that required massive amounts of electricity quickly arrived.

Among the most important was the Carborundum Company, founded in 1891 by inventor Edward Goodrich Acheson. Acheson had discovered how to produce silicon carbide, an extremely hard synthetic material used as an industrial abrasive. The process required furnaces that reached temperatures far hotter than conventional fuel could economically produce. Niagara Falls' hydroelectric power made the process practical on an industrial scale.

Carborundum became one of the city's most famous industrial enterprises. Its abrasives were used to grind steel, sharpen tools, and shape metal parts for factories across the world. During the early twentieth century, the company expanded dramatically, building large production plants along the Niagara River and employing thousands of workers. Its products became essential to the rapidly growing industries of automobiles, machinery, and aviation.

Chemical manufacturing soon followed. One of the most significant companies was Hooker Electrochemical Company, founded by Elon Huntington Hooker. Hooker established large facilities in Niagara Falls in the early twentieth century to take advantage of the region's inexpensive hydroelectric power. Using electrochemical processes, Hooker produced chlorine, caustic soda, and other industrial chemicals that became fundamental components in plastics, pesticides, synthetic materials, and pharmaceuticals.

Hooker's operations expanded rapidly through the first half of the twentieth century, making Niagara Falls one of the largest chemical production centers in the world. The company's products were used in countless industrial applications, and its plants provided thousands of stable union jobs for local residents.

Another major player in the region's chemical industry was Occidental Chemical Corporation, commonly known as OxyChem, which later absorbed Hooker Chemical. OxyChem continued to operate large chlorine and chemical production facilities in Niagara Falls, maintaining the city's long-standing role in the electrochemical industry. These facilities produced essential chemicals used in water purification, plastics manufacturing, and industrial processing.

By the early twentieth century, Niagara Falls had earned the nickname "The Power City." Industrial complexes lined the Niagara River and the power canals. Railroads carried raw materials into the city and shipped finished products across North America. Tourism existed, but it was secondary to the manufacturing economy. This was a union town, where industrial jobs provided stable wages, pensions, and a pathway to the middle class.

Factories also produced paper, rubber products, petrochemicals, abrasives, and metallurgical materials. The city's industries supplied components used in automobiles, electrical equipment, and construction. During World War I and World War II, Niagara Falls factories manufactured chemicals and materials vital to the war effort.

Rapid industrial expansion created challenges as well. Pollution from chemical plants and factories became a significant issue, particularly given the city's proximity to one of the world's great natural landmarks. Yet during the early and mid-twentieth century, economic growth and industrial employment remained the dominant priorities.

By the 1950s and 1960s, however, the industrial landscape began to shift. Technological changes and global competition reduced the advantages of locating factories near hydroelectric power. Many older facilities required expensive modernization, and some companies chose to relocate.

In 1956, the collapse of part of the Niagara Gorge destroyed the Schoellkopf Power Plant.

Opposite: 1960s- Buffalo Avenue

The disaster led to the construction of the Robert Moses Niagara Power Plant in nearby Lewiston, one of the largest hydroelectric generating stations in North America. The new plant secured the region's electricity supply but could not preserve the aging industrial base.

Over the following decades, many factories closed, and manufacturing employment declined. The population of Niagara Falls dropped dramatically as industrial jobs disappeared.

Yet the industrial legacy of Niagara Falls remains profound. Companies like Carborundum, Hooker, and OxyChem helped define the city's identity as a center of innovation in electrochemistry and industrial materials. Their factories transformed Niagara Falls into one of the most important manufacturing centers of the twentieth century.

Today visitors come to see the waterfalls. But for much of the last century, the roar of the Niagara River powered far more than tourism. It powered furnaces, turbines, and factories that helped build the modern industrial world.

OxyChem –August 2021

Shredded Wheat and the Palace of Light

At the turn of the twentieth century, two modern inventions arrived in Niagara Falls at nearly the same moment. One was hydroelectricity, the new and powerful energy harnessed from the roaring river. The other was a

curious breakfast cereal made from whole wheat threads pressed into tidy biscuits. Together they produced one of the most unusual industrial success stories in American food history.

For decades, the factory that made Shredded Wheat became nearly as famous in Niagara Falls as the waterfalls themselves.

The Shredded Wheat Company established its Niagara Falls factory in 1901 along Buffalo Avenue. The location was no accident. Niagara Falls had recently become one of the first cities in the world to harness large-scale hydroelectric power. Electricity generated from the river flowed cheaply and reliably into the growing industrial district along the gorge. For manufacturers requiring large amounts of energy, Niagara Falls offered something rare at the time: abundant power without smoke or coal.

For Henry D. Perky, the inventor of Shredded Wheat, this new energy source was irresistible.

Perky was an Ohio lawyer, entrepreneur, and enthusiastic advocate of the natural health movement. In 1890 he developed Shredded Wheat after searching for a food that could ease his own chronic indigestion. His solution was simple and radical: whole wheat, shredded into fine strands and baked into biscuits without additives or heavy processing. Perky believed deeply that the product had restored his health, and he promoted it as part of a broader philosophy of wholesome living.

But Perky was not merely a health enthusiast. He was also a brilliant marketer.

He understood that building his factory in one of the most famous tourist destinations in the world could help sell his product. Millions already traveled to Niagara Falls to witness the thunder of water plunging over the cliffs. If visitors could also see the creation of a modern health food, they might carry the idea of Shredded Wheat home with them.

The factory that rose along Buffalo Avenue was unlike most industrial buildings of its time.

The five-story structure quickly became known as "The Palace of Light." The nickname was well earned. The building contained nearly 850 windows, allowing sunlight to pour into the production floors through more than 30,000 panes of glass. Natural light filled the factory from morning to evening, reducing the need for artificial lighting and creating a bright, almost cathedral-like interior.

When construction began, the Niagara Gazette captured the public excitement with a headline that read: "It Sounds Like a Dream, Reads Like a

Grain crusher at the Shredded Wheat factory

Fairy Tale, Seems Too Good to Be True."

Perky wanted his factory to be more than a place of machinery and ovens. He envisioned it as a pleasant environment for workers and a showcase for modern industry. Employees enjoyed marble bathroom facilities, a chandeliered lobby, and a company library. The building even included an 800-seat theater, a roof garden overlooking the distant mist of the Falls, and a ballroom where workers could gather for social events.

Outside the factory walls, the landscape was designed by the renowned Olmsted Brothers, heirs to the tradition of Frederick Law Olmsted. Their plan included landscaped walking paths, winding drives, playgrounds, tennis courts, a baseball diamond, and plots where employees could grow vegetables in company gardens. At a time when most factories offered little beyond wages and smoke, these amenities were decades ahead of American corporate thinking.

The plant quickly became one of Niagara Falls' most surprising attractions.

Before factory tours ended in 1946, nearly 100,000 visitors toured the facility each year. The tour became part of the broader marketing of Niagara Falls itself. Travelers who had come to see the waterfalls often added the Shredded Wheat factory to their itinerary. Honeymooners, school groups, and tourists from around the world passed through its bright corridors.

Visitors did more than watch machinery in motion. They attended lectures on diet, cooking, and healthy living. Perky believed that education would inspire people to adopt better habits and purchase his product. Every box of Shredded Wheat reinforced that message, often including statements about health and an image of Niagara Falls itself, turning the famous landscape into an unofficial emblem of the cereal.

In 1950 the company, by then part of Nabisco, moved production to a newer facility on Rainbow Boulevard. The towering silos of the new plant became a landmark in their own right and even appeared in the background of the 1953 film Niagara, starring Marilyn Monroe. Soon afterward, the original Buffalo Avenue "Palace of Light" was demolished.

Yet the connection between Niagara Falls and Shredded Wheat endured. The cereal continued to be produced in the city until 1992. That year, thousands gathered to celebrate the 100th anniversary of the invention that had once linked breakfast tables around the world to the power of the Niagara River.

On a June morning, nearly 12,000 people assembled near the brink of the Falls for a massive commemorative breakfast hosted by television personality Dick Clark. The roar of the water mixed with the clink of cereal bowls.

It was a fitting tribute to a moment when electricity, industry, health ideals, and tourism converged in Niagara Falls to create something unexpectedly enduring: a simple biscuit of wheat and a factory that once shone like glass in the sunlight.

On the Escarpment

The History of Niagara University

Aerial image of Niagara University –1962

If Niagara Falls is built beside thunder, Niagara University is built above it.

Perched along the Niagara Escarpment, overlooking the river that slices its way toward the cataract, Niagara University occupies high ground both literally and historically. Founded in 1856 by the Congregation of the Mission, also known as the Vincentians, the university began as a seminary and college intended to educate young men in faith, discipline, and scholarship.

It was a frontier institution in more ways than one.

A Seminary on the Edge

Mid-nineteenth-century western New York was restless terrain. Industry was emerging. Immigration was accelerating. Catholic communities, many of them Irish and German, sought educational institutions aligned with their faith. Into this environment stepped the Vincentians, disciples of St. Vincent de Paul, whose mission emphasized service, education, and social uplift.

Niagara University began modestly. Its early curriculum focused on classical education, theology, and preparation for priesthood. Latin and philosophy echoed through early classrooms. Discipline was strict. Expectations were high.

The setting mattered

The escarpment offered both physical elevation and symbolic remove. Students studied above the river's turbulence, removed from the commercial noise of the Falls yet close enough to feel its presence. The geography reinforced contemplation.

Expansion and Identity

By the late nineteenth century, Niagara University expanded beyond seminary training to broader collegiate education. As Catholic immigrants settled in western New York and southern Ontario, demand grew for institutions that could educate teachers, lawyers, and

Niagara University Alumni Chapel

professionals within a Catholic framework.

The campus evolved architecturally to match ambition.

Niagara's early buildings were constructed in brick and stone, projecting durability. Over time, Gothic Revival and collegiate architectural elements appeared: pointed arches, quadrangles, and chapel spaces designed to anchor community life. The campus developed a visual identity distinct from the industrial landscape of nearby Niagara Falls.

Faith and scholarship intertwined.

The university's Vincentian identity shaped its ethos. Service to the poor and marginalized became not just theological principle but institutional character. Students were encouraged to see education as preparation for responsibility.

Twentieth-Century Growth

The twentieth century brought transformation.

Enrollment increased steadily, particularly after World War II. Like many American universities, Niagara experienced growth fueled by returning veterans utilizing the GI Bill. Academic programs expanded beyond theology and liberal arts into business, education, and eventually specialized professional fields.

The campus footprint grew accordingly.

Modern academic buildings joined older brick halls. Athletic facilities expanded. Residence halls accommodated a more diverse student body. While the university retained its Catholic foundation, it increasingly served students of varied backgrounds and faiths.

Niagara University adapted to national educational trends while maintaining Vincentian roots.

Cross-Border Influence

Its location near the Canadian border has always shaped the university's identity. Students from Ontario enrolled in significant numbers. Cross-border faculty collaboration occurred naturally. The international dimension, embedded in geography, encouraged broader perspective.

Niagara University's position between Buffalo and Toronto placed it within a regional corridor of commerce and culture. It benefited from proximity to industry while maintaining residential campus character.

The Falls themselves, only minutes away, became informal classroom and retreat space. Students studied beside one of the world's most visible natural wonders, a reminder of scale beyond syllabi.

Coeducation and Modernization

Originally founded as a men's institution, Niagara University gradually embraced coeducation in the twentieth century. The inclusion of women reshaped campus life and academic offerings. Education and nursing programs expanded. The university's culture broadened.

As American higher education professionalized, Niagara invested in accreditation, program development, and faculty scholarship. Business programs gained prominence. Criminal justice and hospitality management reflected regional economic realities.

The institution balanced tradition with adaptation.

Vincentian values remained explicit, but the student experience modernized. Technology entered classrooms. Study abroad programs extended the university's reach. Partnerships with local organizations reinforced its service mission.

Architecture and Atmosphere

Architecturally, Niagara University remains cohesive.

Collegiate brick structures, chapels, and green spaces create a contained environment distinct from the surrounding urban and suburban

Opposite: 1906 - Niagara University

patterns. The campus reads as intentional community rather than scattered facilities. Bell towers and courtyards reinforce identity.

The escarpment location gives the campus both visibility and separation. From certain vantage points, one can glimpse the river valley below, a quiet reminder of the Falls' proximity.

If Niagara Falls the city builds in response to economic cycles, Niagara University builds in response to academic cycles. Additions occur in measured phases. Renovations respect continuity.

The campus architecture expresses stability in a region accustomed to industrial volatility.

Athletics and Identity

Niagara University's athletic programs, particularly basketball and hockey, have contributed to regional identity. The Purple Eagles compete at the Division I level, bringing national visibility and local pride.

Athletic facilities serve not only competition but community. They anchor alumni engagement and foster intergenerational continuity. In a region shaped by cross-border movement and shifting industry, collegiate athletics offer constancy.

Service and Continuity

Through economic downturns, industrial decline, and regional reinvention, Niagara University has persisted. Its Vincentian mission continues to emphasize service and ethical leadership. Students engage in community outreach across Niagara County and beyond.

The university's endurance parallels the broader story of Niagara Falls: adaptation without surrender of core identity.

Where factories closed, the university remained. Where retail thinned, classrooms filled. Education proved more durable than certain industries.

On High Ground

Niagara University occupies physical elevation, but its significance lies in duration.

Founded before the Civil War, it has weathered industrial booms, environmental crises, demographic shifts, and technological revolutions. It has educated clergy, teachers, executives, social workers, and public servants.

It stands above the river not in isolation, but in witness.

The Falls continue their descent.

The city continues its recalibration.

On the escarpment, the university continues its instruction.

Brick, belief, and books.

Built on high ground.

The Challenge *of* Urban Renewal

Cities built beside natural wonders face a peculiar challenge. The landscape draws the world's attention, but the surrounding city must constantly decide what kind of place will frame that spectacle. In Niagara Falls, the decades after World War II brought one of the most dramatic attempts to reshape that relationship through urban renewal.

By the 1950s, Niagara Falls was confronting the same pressures affecting many industrial American cities. Manufacturing jobs that had once powered the local economy were beginning to decline, older neighborhoods showed signs of disinvestment, and civic leaders worried that visitors came to see the waterfalls but spent little time or money in the city itself. Urban renewal promised a solution. Across the United States, planners believed that clearing aging districts and replacing them with modern buildings, wider streets, and large commercial developments would create a cleaner, more prosperous downtown.

The effort accelerated during the 1960s with federal funding provided under the Housing Act of 1949, which allowed cities to purchase and demolish large sections of older property. In Niagara Falls, entire blocks near the tourist district were targeted for clearance. Nineteenth-century houses, small hotels, and locally owned storefronts that had served generations of visitors disappeared in a relatively short period of time. Streets that had once formed a dense urban

Third Avenue at Falls Street

grid were widened or removed altogether as planners imagined a more automobile-oriented downtown.

One of the most ambitious projects was the construction of the Niagara Falls Convention and Civic Center, which opened in 1974 as a 10,000-seat arena and convention facility. Built directly along Falls Street, the structure physically blocked the historic roadway that once connected downtown to Niagara Falls State Park. The project also eliminated portions of Jefferson Avenue and Erie Avenue, two major city thoroughfares. Designed by Philip Johnson and John Burgee, with graphics by Jane Davis Doggett, the building's curved roofline was intended to evoke the rainbow that often forms in the mist of the falls. Locals, however, frequently joked that the structure resembled a giant Quonset hut.

Another centerpiece of the urban renewal strategy was the Rainbow Centre Factory Outlet, a 287,000-square-foot enclosed shopping mall that opened on July 2, 1982. Located at 302 Rainbow Boulevard North, the mall was uniquely designed inside a multilevel parking structure and connected to the former Wintergarden botanical complex. The two-floor indoor mall featured a distinctive central fountain and a mix of national retailers, including Burlington Coat Factory, KB Toys, Waldenbooks, and Cavages, along with a food court intended to serve visiting tourists.

For a time, the concept worked. The mall attracted visitors and briefly succeeded in capturing some of the tourist spending that had historically flowed across the border to Niagara Falls. By 1990 the complex repositioned itself as an outlet center in an effort to remain competitive. But retail patterns were shifting. When the larger Niagara Factory Outlet Mall opened in the nearby Town of Niagara, the Rainbow Centre struggled to keep tenants and eventually closed in 2000.

Opposite: Falls Street demolition

Urban renewal also reshaped the entertainment and tourism landscape. The Convention and Civic Center operated for nearly three decades before closing in 2002. The site was soon redeveloped as the Seneca Niagara Resort & Casino, reflecting a new era of tourism built around gaming and large resort development. Across the street, the modern Niagara Falls Convention Center opened in 2004 on Old Falls Street, providing more than 116,000 square feet of exhibition and meeting space.

Even the Rainbow Centre found a second life. After years of vacancy, the building was donated to SUNY Niagara in 2010 and transformed into the Niagara Falls Culinary Institute, which opened in 2012 along with a Barnes & Noble bookstore.

Urban renewal in Niagara Falls produced mixed results. Modern buildings replaced aging ones, but the process also erased historic neighborhoods and displaced longtime residents. Some of the promised redevelopment arrived slowly, leaving empty parcels where busy streets had once stood.

Yet the story is not entirely one of loss. While the city experimented with new commercial strategies, the natural landscape itself remained protected within the park system first envisioned by Frederick Law Olmsted in the nineteenth century. The waterfalls continued their endless descent, unchanged by the shifting architecture around them.

Urban renewal at Niagara Falls ultimately reveals the complicated balance between preservation, tourism, and economic survival. The city cleared space in hopes of building a new future. Some of that future arrived. Some of it took different forms than planners imagined. But like the river that gathers momentum before the brink, the effort reflected a persistent belief that the city beside the falls could still reinvent itself.

STOP
THIRD ST

Love Canal

The Toxic Legacy Beneath a Neighborhood

The neighborhood looked ordinary.

Ranch houses. Chain-link fences. Swing sets pressed into small backyards. On humid summer evenings, the air carried the scent of cut grass and something else people struggled to name.

Love Canal was never meant to be a neighborhood.

In the 1890s, entrepreneur William T. Love hoped to give his name to history as an epic city builder and energy titan. Love arrived in the Niagara Falls region convinced that the roaring Niagara River could power a new kind of industrial metropolis. He called the vision Model City, a planned community stretching across thousands of acres between Lake Erie and Lake Ontario.

Love imagined a city of clean factories powered by hydroelectric energy, surrounded by affordable housing, parks, and modern infrastructure. Electricity, telephones, sewer systems, and even pneumatic mail delivery would serve residents. At a time when American cities struggled with overcrowding and pollution, Love promised something different. Model City, he said, would be "the most perfect city in existence."

The key to the plan was a canal.

Love proposed digging a waterway that would divert water from the upper Niagara River, carry it inland, and return it downstream after passing through turbines that would generate power for factories and homes. The project began with enormous optimism. In 1894, Love and his investors gathered for groundbreaking ceremonies at the canal site near the village of LaSalle. Steam

1894 – William T. Love at the Love Canal groundbreaking.

excavators, mule teams, and laborers began carving a trench through clay and shale.

For a moment, the dream seemed possible.

Then the financial world shifted beneath it. The Panic of 1893 had already shaken investor confidence, and the costs of acquiring land began to rise as speculation spread across Niagara County. At the same time, advances in long-distance electrical transmission made it possible to send hydroelectric power farther from Niagara Falls without constructing massive canals. The canal became less necessary.

By 1896, Love's finances collapsed. Work stopped after only about 3,000 feet of the canal had been excavated. The ambitious project dissolved into lawsuits, unpaid debts, and abandoned machinery. All that remained was a long trench cutting across the landscape.

For decades, the canal simply sat there.

Rainwater collected in it. Weeds and trees grew along its edges. Local children swam in the water during the summer and skated across the frozen surface in winter. The failed industrial dream slowly faded from memory.

Industry eventually discovered another use for the abandoned trench.

Between 1942 and 1953, the Hooker Chemical Company began using the canal as a disposal site for chemical waste generated by its Niagara Falls plants. Steel drums filled with solvents, pesticides, and other industrial byproducts were buried in layers. The site was sealed with clay and soil, and by the time dumping ended more than 21,000 tons of chemical waste had been placed in the canal.

In 1953, Hooker sold the land to the Niagara Falls Board of Education for one dollar, warning in the deed that hazardous materials were buried there.

Development followed anyway.

The 99th Street School was built near the canal, and new housing developments quickly surrounded the site. By the late 1950s, hundreds of families lived in the neighborhood. To residents, it appeared to be a quiet working-class suburb.

For years, nothing seemed unusual.

Then the ground began to speak.

Heavy rains and snowmelt during the 1970s raised groundwater levels and pushed buried chemicals toward the surface. Oily substances appeared in yards and basements. Strange odors drifted through homes. Children sometimes returned from playing outside with burns or unexplained rashes.

93rd Street School

Residents began comparing stories. Illnesses that once seemed isolated started forming patterns. Birth defects, miscarriages, cancers, and respiratory problems appeared at troubling rates. A young resident named Lois Gibbs began organizing neighbors after her son developed health problems at the nearby school. Her door-to-door survey revealed a disturbing cluster of illnesses across the community.

DANGER
HAZARDOUS
WASTE AREA
UNAUTHORIZED
PERSONNEL
KEEP OUT
NEW YORK STATE DEPARTMENT OF
ENVIRONMENTAL CONSERVATION
1-800-342-9296

In 1978, state investigators confirmed the danger. More than 200 chemical compounds were found in the soil and groundwater, including benzene and dioxin.

That year, New York Governor Hugh Carey declared a public health emergency and ordered evacuations for the families living closest to the canal. Two years later, President Jimmy Carter issued the first federal emergency declaration for a human-made environmental disaster.

Love Canal had become a national symbol.

The crisis led directly to the passage of the Comprehensive Environmental Response, Compensation, and Liability Act, commonly known as Superfund. The law created a federal program to identify and clean up hazardous waste sites across the country.

Cleanup at Love Canal took decades.

Contaminated soil was removed, drainage systems were installed, and sections of the neighborhood were eventually redeveloped.

Yet the name never escaped its past.

What began as William Love's utopian canal for a perfect industrial city ended as one of the most famous environmental disasters in American history. The trench dug for progress became a warning about the hidden costs of industrial ambition.

For decades the earth kept its secrets.

Eventually, it spoke.

From Collapse to Continuity

Hydropower After Schoellkopf

On June 7, 1956, the Niagara Gorge delivered a stark reminder that even the most confident engineering must ultimately answer to geology. When the Schoellkopf Hydroelectric Station *(above)* collapsed into the river below, the event was more than a tragic industrial accident. It marked the end of one era of power generation at Niagara Falls and forced the beginning of another.

For decades, the Schoellkopf station had been one of the major producers of hydroelectric power along the Niagara River. Built in stages beginning in the late nineteenth century by industrialist Jacob F. Schoellkopf, the plant clung dramatically to the steep walls of the Niagara Gorge. Water diverted from the river above the falls plunged through tunnels and penstocks, spinning turbines that supplied electricity to factories and communities across Western New York.

The facility was both an engineering achievement and a symbol of Niagara Falls' industrial identity. Rows of brick buildings and steel structures lined the gorge wall just downstream from the American Falls, capturing the river's immense energy. Yet the same geology that made Niagara Falls spectacular also made the site vulnerable. The gorge is formed from layers of limestone resting on softer shale, and over time water seeped into the rock, weakening the cliff behind the plant.

On that summer afternoon in 1956, a large section of the cliff suddenly gave way. The rock collapse triggered a chain reaction that destroyed portions of the power station. Within minutes, buildings and machinery slid into the turbulent river below. Eleven workers lost their lives in the disaster, and the region suddenly lost one of its major sources of electrical generation.

Even before the collapse, however, engineers had begun planning the next stage of hydroelectric development along the Niagara River. The disaster accelerated those plans dramatically.

Within months, New York State moved forward with construction of a much larger and more modern hydroelectric facility. Named after the powerful public official who had championed the development of the river's resources, the Robert Moses Niagara Power Plant would become the centerpiece of a new era of energy production.

Construction began in 1958, just two years after the Schoellkopf disaster. Unlike the earlier plants that clung to the gorge walls, the new station was built on stable ground farther downstream. Massive intake structures diverted water from the Niagara River into underground tunnels that carried it to enormous turbines before releasing it back into the lower river.

Completed in 1961, the Robert Moses Niagara Power Plant *(Opposite)* became one of the largest hydroelectric generating stations in North America. It was paired with the nearby Lewiston Pump-Generating Plant, which introduced pumped-storage technology to the Niagara power system.

During periods of low electricity demand, water from the Niagara River is pumped into a large reservoir above the Lewiston facility. When demand increases, the stored water is released through turbines, generating additional power when it is most needed. This system allows operators to balance supply and demand while making efficient use of the river's energy.

The new complex reshaped the power landscape of Niagara Falls. Instead of several smaller stations scattered along the gorge, electricity generation became concentrated in large, modern facilities designed with greater attention to geological stability and safety.

Today, the Robert Moses Niagara Power Plant *(Opposite)*remains one of the largest sources of renewable electricity in New York State. Alongside Canadian facilities such as the Sir Adam Beck stations, it forms part of an international system that carefully balances energy production with the preservation of the world-famous waterfalls.

The collapse of the Schoellkopf station was a devastating moment in the history of Niagara Falls. Yet it also marked a turning point. From the ruins of the old gorge-side plant emerged a new generation of hydroelectric engineering capable of harnessing the power of the Niagara River more safely and efficiently.

The river continues to rush toward the falls with the same relentless force it has carried for thousands of years. Today that force not only inspires awe, but also lights homes and powers communities across the region.

The roar of Niagara is no longer only a sound of nature.

It is the sound of power.

The Day Niagara Falls Ran Dry

For centuries Niagara Falls has been defined by thunder. The constant roar of water plunging into the Niagara Gorge is so powerful that visitors often feel the vibration beneath their feet. Yet in the summer of 1969, something extraordinary happened: for the first time in modern history, the American Falls fell silent.

Niagara Falls is one of the most powerful waterfalls on Earth. Every minute, roughly 4.5 million gallons of water pour over the American Falls and Bridal Veil Falls, creating the iconic spectacle that draws millions of visitors each year. But concerns about the long-term stability of the American Falls led scientists and engineers to take an unprecedented step: temporarily turning the waterfall off.

The American Falls is smaller than the

neighboring Horseshoe Falls, but it is geologically complex. Over centuries, enormous chunks of limestone and dolomite had broken away from the cliff face, creating a massive talus pile of boulders at the base. By the late 1960s, geologists worried that continued rockfalls could dramatically alter the falls, perhaps even causing them to erode into a steep cascade rather than the dramatic drop visitors expected.

To investigate the situation, the International Joint Commission, the body that manages shared water resources between the United States and Canada, approved an ambitious plan. Engineers would temporarily divert the Niagara River away from the American Falls so that scientists could study the exposed rock face and determine how to stabilize it.

The project began on June 9, 1969, when crews constructed a massive temporary dam upstream. Over three days, more than **1,200 truckloads of rock—nearly 28,000 tons—**were dumped into the river to form a 600-foot-wide cofferdam stretching from Goat Island to the mainland. The structure redirected the flow of the Niagara River away from the American Falls and toward the much larger Horseshoe Falls on the Canadian side.

Within hours, the thunderous curtain of water shrank to a trickle.

For the first time in thousands of years, the rocky cliff of the American Falls stood exposed. Photographers and journalists flocked to the scene, capturing images that seemed almost surreal: the famous waterfall reduced to bare stone and scattered streams. Visitors could see details normally hidden behind the rushing water, including deep cracks in the rock and the enormous pile of fallen boulders at the base.

The U.S. Army Corps of Engineers immediately began a detailed geological investigation. Crews drilled into the cliff to measure stresses and faults within the rock. Instruments were installed to monitor movement, and engineers carefully mapped the layers of limestone and shale that make up the escarpment.

Stabilization work followed. Steel bolts and cables were installed to secure unstable sections of rock near Luna Island and Bridal Veil Falls, while

drainage holes were drilled to relieve hydrostatic pressure trapped within the cliff. Engineers also examined whether the talus pile should be removed to restore the original vertical drop of the waterfall.

The dry riverbed also produced unexpected discoveries. Two human bodies were found among the rocks, a grim reminder of Niagara's long history of accidents and suicides. Tourists exploring the exposed area also collected coins that had been tossed into the water over decades.

After months of study, engineers reached an important conclusion. Removing the massive boulder field at the base of the American Falls would be extremely expensive and potentially destabilizing. Instead, they recommended allowing nature to take its course, while reinforcing areas of the cliff that showed signs of weakness.

By November 1969, the work was complete. The temporary dam was dismantled, and the waters of the Niagara River were released once again. Gradually, the familiar roar returned as water cascaded over the American Falls.

Since that remarkable summer, the waterfall has flowed uninterrupted. The dramatic experiment of 1969 remains one of the most unusual chapters in Niagara Falls history—a moment when one of the world's greatest natural wonders briefly fell silent so that science could better understand how to preserve it.

Water shapes stone.

Economy shapes architecture.

Built Beside the Brink

The Architecture of Niagara Falls

Niagara Falls has never been a city that builds quietly. When you live beside one of the loudest natural features on the continent, subtlety feels optional. The architecture here answers the roar with posture. Brick, limestone, terra cotta, steel, and glass rise not in imitation of the Falls, but in conversation with them.

The built environment of Niagara Falls tells the story of tourism and industry, ambition and retreat, spectacle and recalibration. It is not architecturally uniform. It is layered. Victorian elegance stands near mid-century mass. Adaptive reuse shares blocks with vacancy. The skyline has shifted with every economic tide.

To read Niagara Falls architecturally is to read its eras.

The Grand Gesture: Hotels and the Framing of Wonder

As tourism accelerated in the nineteenth century, Niagara Falls began constructing architecture worthy of its attraction. Visitors did not simply want proximity to the cataract. They wanted ceremony.

Hotels like the Cataract House *(below)* rose in stages beginning in 1825, expanding into sprawling complexes with columned verandas and grand dining rooms. These were buildings that performed hospitality. Italianate details, mansard roofs, ornamental cornices, and wide porches framed the landscape. Architecture became a lens through which visitors consumed awe.

Many of these early hotel structures are gone, victims of fire or redevelopment. But their impulse endures: Niagara Falls builds for drama.

Civic Confidence: The United Office Building

In 1929, on the eve of the Great Depression, Niagara Falls reached upward.

The United Office Building, rising fourteen stories above downtown, remains one of the city's most recognizable landmarks. Designed by architect James A. Johnson of the Buffalo firm Esenwein & Johnson, the structure reflects the confident architectural language of the late Art Deco period. Its strong vertical lines, stepped setbacks, and ornamental detailing give the

United Office Building

building a sense of upward motion, a visual expression of ambition. Terra cotta panels and stylized decorative motifs capture the spirit of the late 1920s, when Niagara Falls imagined itself not only as an industrial powerhouse but as an emerging corporate center.

In the decades that followed, downtown retail gradually thinned and many offices emptied as economic patterns shifted. Yet the United Office Building endured.

The Era of Enclosure: Rainbow Centre and Reinvention

In 1978, the Rainbow Centre Mall introduced enclosed retail modernism to downtown Niagara Falls. Concrete and glass replaced brick storefront rhythms. Climate control replaced sidewalk engagement.

The architecture turned inward. For a time, the mall symbolized adaptation to changing retail trends. But as anchor tenants departed and regional competition intensified, the structure's vast interior spaces felt isolated rather than invigorating. Portions were eventually demolished, leaving behind a lesson in scale without sustained density.

Its lifecycle reflects Niagara Falls' architectural experimentation during late twentieth-century transition.

The Glass Garden: Wintergarden

Completed in 2010, the Wintergarden *(opposite)* introduced a different architectural vocabulary to Niagara Falls: transparency. The enclosed glass atrium spans Rainbow Boulevard, connecting the Seneca Niagara Resort & Casino to the former convention center. Filled with trees and natural light, the space functions as an indoor streetscape, blending public movement with climate-controlled comfort. It reflects a contemporary effort to merge urban continuity with visitor convenience.

The name, however, reaches back to an earlier and far more ambitious vision. The original Niagara Falls Wintergarden opened in 1977 as a cornerstone of downtown revitalization. Designed by world-renowned modernist architect César Pelli, the dramatic 110-foot-high glass enclosure was conceived as a year-round attraction, a tropical sanctuary in the heart of the city. Inside, visitors encountered a multi-level botanical park filled with ponds, a waterfall, and more than 7,000 trees. The contrast between the snowy streets outside and the lush greenery within made the building a stunning tour de force. It was architectural poetry.

The Wintergarden was never intended to generate profit. Instead, it was offered as a public amenity, a welcoming civic gateway. Over time, however, its role changed. In 2003 the property was sold for one million dollars to a private enterprise. The tropical garden disappeared, replaced by Smokin' Joe Anderson's Family Fun Center. By November 2007 the building closed, and raised ending an unusual chapter in the city's architectural and cultural life.

Opposite: Niagara Falls Wintergarden

Public Art and Symbol: The Niagara Falls Turtle

The Turtle, also known as the Native American Center for the Living Arts, stands as a striking symbol of Indigenous heritage and cultural renewal. Completed in 1981 and designed by Arapaho architect Dennis Sun Rhodes, the building's distinctive turtle-shaped form was inspired by the Haudenosaunee creation story in which Sky Woman lands upon the back of a turtle, giving rise to the land known as Turtle Island.

Constructed just fifteen years after the closure of the last federally funded Indian boarding school in the United States, the center represented a powerful moment of cultural reclamation. At a time when Indigenous communities across the country were working to revive languages, traditions, and artistic expression that had been suppressed for generations, the Turtle emerged as a place dedicated to education, cultural preservation, and healing. Located near the brink of Niagara Falls, it quickly became an important gathering space where visitors could learn about Indigenous history, art, and philosophy.

The center featured exhibitions, performances, and educational programming that celebrated Native American creativity and identity. For a time, it was recognized as the largest Indigenous arts center in the eastern United States, drawing artists, scholars, and visitors interested in exploring the rich cultural traditions of Native nations.

Despite its cultural significance, the center faced ongoing financial challenges. In 1996, after fifteen years of operation, the Native American Center for the Living Arts closed its doors. Not long afterward, the property was purchased by a private developer. Since then, the building has remained vacant for nearly three decades.

Over the years, proposals have surfaced that would dramatically change the site. At one point, the owner outlined plans to demolish the structure and replace it with a high-rise hotel overlooking Niagara Falls. Meanwhile, alterations to the building itself have made its original design more difficult to recognize. The bold, multicolored stripes that once emphasized the Turtle's sculptural, zoomorphic form have been painted white, muting the visual impact envisioned by its architect.

Today the building stands in an uncertain state. Although widely recognized for its cultural symbolism and architectural uniqueness, the Turtle is not protected as a local landmark. Its future remains unresolved, leaving an important piece of Indigenous cultural history in limbo.

Even in its quiet state, however, the Turtle continues to represent something larger than the structure itself. It embodies a moment in time when Indigenous artists, educators, and leaders sought to create a place of visibility and pride at one of the most visited natural sites in the world. Whether preserved, restored, or lost to redevelopment, the story of the Turtle remains an important chapter in the cultural landscape of Niagara Falls.

Architecture as Memory

Niagara Falls architecture is not unified by a single style. It oscillates between Victorian ornament, Romanesque solidity, Art Deco ambition, modernist utility, suburban pragmatism, and contemporary glass.

The United Office Building reaches upward in 1920s optimism.

The Wintergarden gleamed in transparency.

The turtle rests in symbolic continuity.

Each structure marks an economic and cultural chapter.

And through it all, the Falls continue their descent, indifferent to facade treatments or zoning maps.

Niagara Falls builds knowing permanence is provisional.

Water carves the gorge.

Architecture carves the skyline.

Gaming the Mist

When factories close, cities look for engines.

By the late twentieth century, Niagara Falls had lost much of the industrial base that once defined it. The turbines still spun at the edge of town. The water still fell. But payrolls had thinned, storefronts had darkened, and the city faced a familiar post-industrial question: What comes next?

The answer arrived not in brick and smokestacks, but in glass and neon.

In 2002, the Seneca Niagara Resort & Casino opened on land owned by the Seneca Nation of Indians. The project emerged from a gaming compact negotiated between the Seneca Nation and New York State, granting the Nation exclusive rights to operate casinos in certain regions of western New York.

The development altered the skyline overnight.

A hotel tower rose where industrial structures once dominated. Parking garages replaced vacant lots. The glow from the casino's façade joined the long-standing illumination of the Falls themselves. For the first time in decades, cranes returned to the skyline not to dismantle, but to build.

The casino promised jobs and revenue.

Hundreds of positions opened in hospitality, security, gaming operations, and food service. For some residents, employment returned within city limits. For municipal leaders, gaming revenue offered relief to strained budgets. The compact provided financial flows to both the Seneca Nation and the state, with host community payments directed toward local government.

But gaming is not industry.

Casinos function differently from factories. They draw visitors for shorter stays. They concentrate activity within controlled interiors. They generate excitement and revenue, but not necessarily broad-based economic spillover. The challenge became how to translate foot traffic into sustained downtown vitality.

The city attempted alignment.

Streetscape improvements followed. Hotels and chain restaurants clustered nearby. Marketing emphasized proximity to the Falls and cross-border access to Ontario's established tourism infrastructure. The Rainbow Bridge carried not only pedestrians but economic calculation.

Yet reliance on gaming carried its own vulnerability.

Revenue fluctuations tied to economic cycles and border policies introduced unpredictability. Disputes between the Seneca Nation and the state periodically interrupted host payments, straining municipal finances. The relationship required ongoing negotiation, balancing sovereignty, partnership, and local dependency.

Sovereignty added dimension.

The Seneca Nation's presence in the Niagara region predates the city itself. The gaming compact represented modern expression of Indigenous economic autonomy. The casino was not simply commercial enterprise. It was assertion of self-determination within a legal framework shaped by federal Indian law.

Niagara Falls thus entered a new phase, one in which economic strategy intersected with historic claims to land and authority.

Meanwhile, tourism diversified.

The Falls remained central attraction, drawing millions annually. Illumination technology advanced. Fireworks punctuated summer nights. Festivals and seasonal events attempted to extend visitor stays. Investments in park infrastructure aimed to improve the experience without overwhelming it.

The city also pursued smaller-scale redevelopment efforts: adaptive reuse of historic buildings, promotion of local restaurants, encouragement of niche retail. Progress was incremental. Post-industrial landscapes rarely transform in a single wave.

Hydropower continued quietly in the background.

The New York Power Authority maintained its generating capacity at the Robert Moses Niagara Power Plant, providing renewable electricity to the regional grid. The city remained energy producer even as its local economy leaned more heavily toward hospitality and entertainment.

The contrast was striking.

On one side of town, turbines spun within concrete vaults. On the other, slot machines chimed beneath chandeliers. Both converted flow into revenue, one through gravity, the other through risk.

Gaming did not solve every structural challenge facing Niagara Falls. Poverty rates remained high. Population stabilized but did not rebound dramatically. Some blocks thrived while others struggled.

But the casino signaled something important.

It demonstrated that reinvention was possible. That the skyline need not reflect only loss. That partnership, even complicated partnership, could generate movement.

Niagara Falls has always negotiated with power.

First geological. Then industrial. Now economic and sovereign.

The mist still rises over the gorge. The lights still shift across the cascade at night. Beneath them, a city continues the long work of adaptation, wagering that momentum can be built from whatever force is available.

The water falls without pause.

The city keeps finding ways to respond.

Living Next Door to Wonder

Most visitors never see it.

They park. They walk toward the sound. They photograph the brink. They leave.

For millions each year, Niagara Falls, New York is a railing, a poncho, a rainbow. The city becomes backdrop to the waterfall, a necessary but secondary frame. Hotels are remembered. Restaurants are reviewed. The neighborhood streets just beyond the park boundary blur into peripheral vision.

But the city behind the Falls is not peripheral to itself.

It is residential blocks where porch lights flick on at dusk. It is corner stores with handwritten signs. It is schools that open each September regardless of tourism season. It is churches that hold weddings in winter when visitor traffic thins and snow banks press against stained glass.

The spectacle generates headlines. The neighborhoods generate continuity.

Niagara Falls grew in concentric layers. Early settlement clustered near the river and portage routes. Industrial expansion stretched development eastward along Buffalo Avenue. Worker housing followed factory footprints. Ethnic enclaves formed around parishes and clubs. Each wave left architecture and memory.

When industry contracted, the built environment remained.

Vacant factories cast long shadows over streets where families had built generational lives. Some houses emptied. Others persisted. In certain neighborhoods, vacancy spread unevenly, block by block. On one street, lawns were

trimmed and gardens tended. Around the corner, windows boarded.

This unevenness defines the modern city more accurately than any single statistic.

Poverty rates remain higher than state averages. Median incomes reflect decades of economic contraction. Yet numbers cannot fully describe daily resilience. Residents organize block clubs. Schools pursue partnerships. Local entrepreneurs attempt storefront revival.

The border complicates identity.

Across the river, Niagara Falls, Ontario presents a skyline dense with hotels and attractions. The Canadian side's tourism infrastructure often overshadows its American counterpart in scale. The comparison is inevitable and frequently unkind. But comparison can obscure distinct character.

The American side is less spectacle-driven, more residential in texture. Its skyline is punctuated by the tower of the Seneca Niagara Resort & Casino, but beyond that vertical marker lies a grid of streets shaped by industrial era planning.

Community anchors endure.

High schools graduate classes that often remain connected through extended family networks. Churches host food drives and festivals. Nonprofit organizations address housing insecurity and youth programming. The civic ecosystem operates quietly, outside the gaze of tourists.

There is also pride.

Ask longtime residents what defines Niagara Falls and many will not begin with tourism brochures. They will speak of neighbors who stayed when others left. They will recall factory shifts and union halls. They will reference the river not as postcard but as constant companion.

The Falls are magnificent. The city is practical.

Urban challenges remain visible. Infrastructure requires maintenance. Public schools face funding pressures. Efforts at downtown revitalization proceed in cycles of optimism and recalibration. Demolition of derelict properties clears space but can also leave voids awaiting purpose.

Yet there is something steady in the presence of the water.

Children grow up hearing the distant roar as ambient sound. It becomes background to homework and dinner conversations. The extraordinary normalizes. Living beside a world-renowned waterfall does not eliminate daily concerns about employment, housing, or healthcare. It simply layers them with an unusual horizon.

Niagara Falls, New York is not defined solely by what spills over stone. It is defined by who remains after the tour buses depart.

In recent years, efforts to reconnect neighborhoods with the waterfront have gained momentum. Investments in streetscape improvements and small business development seek to bridge the gap between park and city. The goal is not to compete with the waterfall, but to complement it.

Identity at the edge is complicated.

The city must negotiate between external perception and internal reality. It must honor industrial legacy without being trapped by it. It must leverage tourism without becoming caricature.

Behind the Falls lies a community that has weathered expansion, contamination, contraction, and reinvention. It has absorbed comparison and critique. It continues to educate children, repair roofs, and shovel snow in winter.

Visitors see water in motion.

Residents see seasons.

The city behind the Falls does not roar. It persists.

And persistence, in a place shaped by such force, is its own kind of power.

Flowing Forward

Cities rarely tell their stories in straight lines. They tell them in layers.

Niagara Falls is one of those places where history settles like the rock strata of the gorge itself: limestone resting on shale, each layer recording a different moment in time. The city that grew beside the falls was shaped by the same slow accumulation of events. Industry rose, fortunes were made and lost, neighborhoods expanded, and visitors arrived from around the world, each generation believing it was encountering the falls for the first time.

The water, of course, does not notice.

For thousands of years the Niagara River has flowed north from Lake Erie to Lake Ontario, carving its path through ancient rock. The gorge beneath the falls is not simply scenery but a record of time in motion. Long before the first mills turned or the first railroads reached the region, the river had already begun shaping the landscape that would eventually draw the world's attention.

What changed over time was not the river, but how people understood it.

To Indigenous communities, the Niagara River was a living corridor of trade, travel, and meaning. It was part of a landscape that connected the Great Lakes and the people who lived along their shores. To early European explorers, the falls were both a natural wonder and a barrier that forced travelers to carry their goods along the portage path around the rapids.

By the nineteenth century, a different idea began to take hold. The same force that produced the spectacle of the falls could also produce power. Entrepreneurs and engineers began to imagine ways to harness the river's energy. Canals were cut, turbines were installed, and factories rose along the banks. Niagara Falls became one of the first places in the world where large-scale hydroelectric power transformed water into electricity.

The city grew alongside that transformation.

Hotels and observation towers welcomed visitors who came to witness the famous cataract. Streetcars connected neighborhoods to factories and scenic viewpoints. Railroads delivered thousands of travelers each year. Niagara Falls became a place where industry and tourism lived side by side, each shaping the identity of the city.

Yet the falls themselves remained larger than any single plan.

They survived economic booms and industrial decline. They endured rockfalls, winter ice, and the steady erosion that continues to reshape the gorge. Even the boldest engineering projects—diverting water for power, stabilizing cliffs, or temporarily draining the American Falls for study—have always been temporary gestures beside a landscape still in motion.

Nature continues to write the long story here.

Today Niagara Falls stands at another moment of balance. Hydroelectric plants quietly generate electricity for millions of homes. At the same time, visitors from around the world gather along the railings of Niagara Falls State Park to watch the water plunge into the gorge below. The same river that once powered early mills now fuels a modern renewable energy system while still inspiring awe in those who come to see it.

The river performs both roles without effort.

It powers cities. It inspires wonder.

And perhaps that is the enduring lesson of Niagara Falls. The story of this place is not simply about industry or tourism, or even about a famous waterfall. It is about a community learning, generation after generation, how to live beside one of the most powerful natural forces on the continent.

About the Author

Mark Donnelly, PhD., is a former marketing professor, history geek, photographer, and creative instigator with more than 60 books to his name. He is best known as the graybeard lecturer who turned a squeaky whiteboard and an alarming intake of coffee into a teaching philosophy built on clarity, curiosity, and retelling the human experience.

Dr. Donnelly built his reputation the old-fashioned way: by simplifying the truth. Not the buzzword-heavy, corporate-approved version, but the real kind that only emerges after watching trends rise, fall, and reappear wearing different shoes. His work is grounded in the belief that complexity is often a failure of explanation, not intelligence, and that understanding should feel empowering, not exclusive.

Throughout academia, Donnelly also wandered productively through newspapers, publishing, consulting, community development, and philanthropic strategy. Along the way, he collected stories, scars, insights, and more thrift-store books than any one man reasonably needs. That varied path informs his teaching and writing style: part historian, part storyteller, part field guide for navigating change without losing your footing.

As a writer, Donnelly moves easily between disciplines, connecting marketing to neuroscience, history to culture, and cities to the people who build them. His historical work, particularly on Western New York, reflects the same sensibility as his teaching: respect for lived experience, skepticism of easy narratives, and deep interest in how people adapt when the ground shifts beneath them.

He lives and creates in Kenmore, New York, with his bride, Princess Laura, surrounded by an ever-growing pile of notebooks, half-finished ideas, and books he swears he's going to write next.

His lifelong principle remains simple: Make a difference.

This book is his latest attempt to do exactly that.

www.ingramcontent.com/pod-product-compliance
Lightning Source LLC
LaVergne TN
LVHW060601110826
845154LV00004B/106

9781956688719